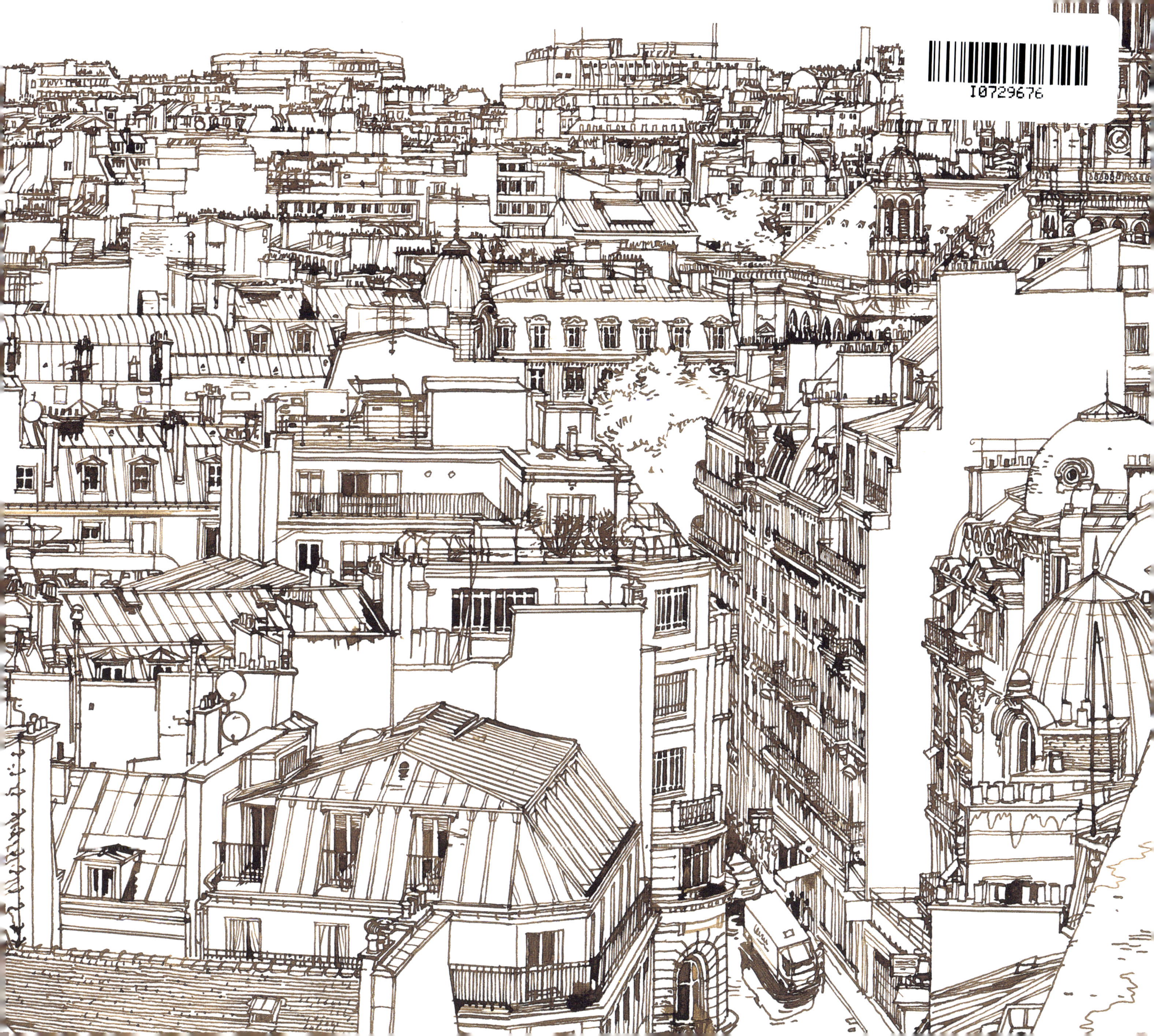
I0729676

ROOFTOPS OF PARIS

sketchbook

This volume has been in print for
a number of years, even decades,
and continues to enchant readers.
While some of the places mentioned
may have changed or closed during
this time, and some of the text
may seem dated, this re-edition
prolongs the atmosphere that
was, and still is, unique to Paris.

© Fabrice Moireau (watercolours)
© Carl Norac (text)

© Les Éditions du Pacifique, 2023
29, rue des Trois Bornes, 75011 Paris
www.leseditionsdupacifique.com

Collection manager: Marie-Claude Millet

First published: 2010 as *Toits de Paris*

This edition:
Editing: Françoise Mathay
Design and typesetting: Benoit Dupré

The illustration on pages 40-41 is
reproduced with the permission of the
Musée du Quai Branly - Jacques Chirac.

All rights reserved.
ISBN: 978-2-87868-282-3

Printed à Saint-Just-la-Pendue
by Imprimerie Chirat, France
on Fedrigoni Arena Natural
Bulk Blanc FSC paper

Legal deposit: April 2023

Cover:
View of the rooftops of Paris
from the Centre Georges-Pompidou.

Below:
27 Boulevard Poissonnière,
the former home of Frédéric Chopin.

Title page:
Workshops on Rue Ménilmontant,
Belleville.

Back cover:
Fabrice Moireau sketching
while seated on a Paris rooftop.

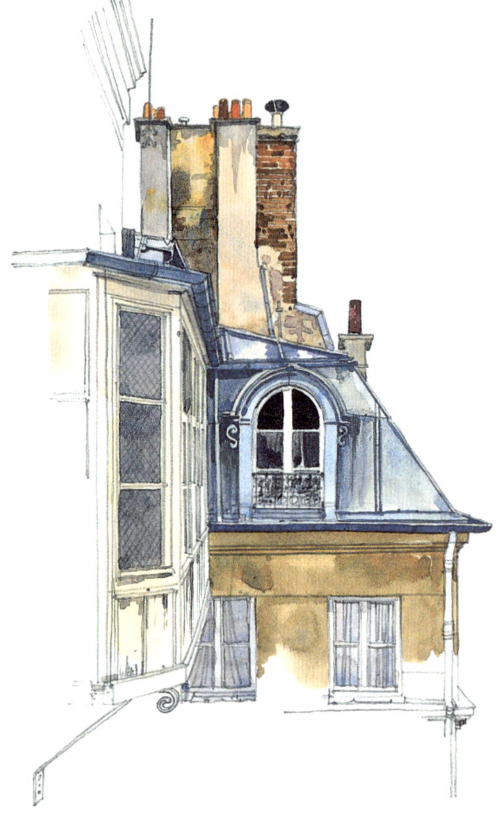

ROOFTOPS OF PARIS

sketchbook

PAINTINGS FABRICE MOIREAU
TEXT CARL NORAC

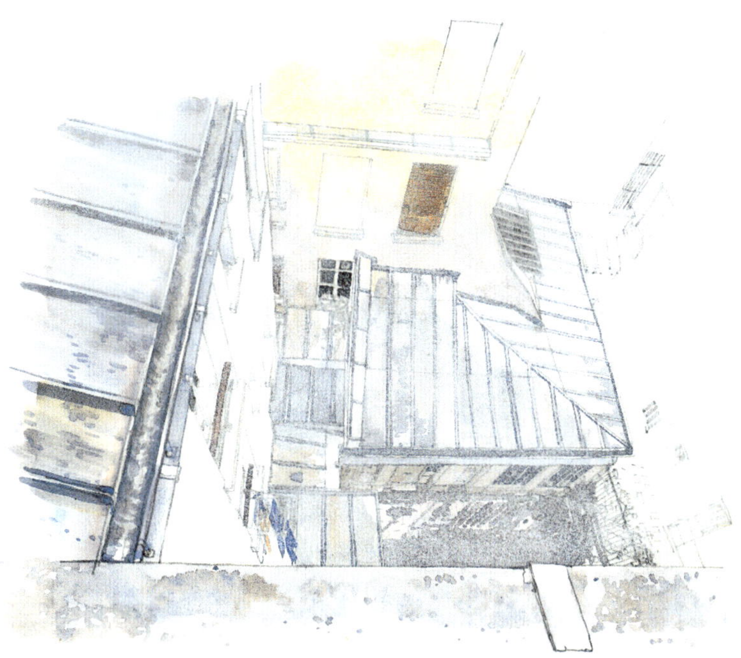

Les Éditions du Pacifique

Paris on high

The rooftops of Paris have always been able to capture the imagination. They make up a landscape with which we feel familiar, and yet we barely know it. Books on Paris are legion. There are virtually none devoted to its rooftops, a fact which tends to support Jean Follain's elegant description of a city conceived from the roots upwards rather than from the roofs down: "The houses of Paris stand... magnificently wedded to the earth, to animal life at ground level, to the fauna of the deep. People live and die behind their grey windows."

This Paris, fixed, rooted, does exist, earthly and resplendent, but up on the rooftops there is a different world, a world of free forms where secrets reveal themselves to eyes patient enough to look. The idea behind this book was to bring to life the roofscape of Paris through the detail of watercolour, with paintings accompanied by text that goes beyond prosaic description to capture some of the poetic imaginings inspired by these rooftops, by what they tell us and what they hide.

The artist Fabrice Moireau undertook a close study of the city surveying it at roof level, with an entomologist's eye for detail. He went around slipping into apartment complexes, pretending to live in the buildings, and, taking opportunities as they presented themselves, climbed up to paint views while perched on high vantage points liable to give anyone vertigo. He wanted to include the city's lesser known nooks and crannies alongside the famous buildings and public places, with new ways of seeing and unusual angles. He is fascinated by this other side of Paris, a levitated, almost unreal world and its architecture devoid of grandiose statements, an extravagant, almost unbelievable mass of shapes and forms and ingenious methods of giving protection from rain, wind and architectural monotony.

This book is an invitation to travel to a new and unfamiliar cityscape. For the artist, this entailed learning to read the roofs of Paris and decipher when they were built, the language of shapes, the game of identifying monuments from afar, set on a 360-degree horizon. And to experience the way in which colours merge and mingle, creating new and subtle intermediate shades, improvised and cheerfully harmonious.

As a watercolourist, Fabrice Moireau is also an explorer. The movement of his paintbrush is sometimes controlled, at other times more spontaneous. He picks up his distinctive case, and a little container of water, then takes to the roofs. Right up there, high above the city for longer periods even than a bird, his brush flying across the rough-textured paper, he seizes the moment with the spirit of a wanderer. Fabrice walks across roofs with a smile in his heart, delighted to have rung at the doors of strangers, to have persevered up meandering staircases, to have found the perfect window with its precious shaft of light. He sits for four or five hours at a time, eyes riveted but paintbrush and palette at work, fulfilling his mission to share with us what the eye sees, to present the images that are right in front of us.

For the poet, too, the roofs are like manna from heaven, bringing him or her into a world full of fleeting silhouettes and the music of birdsong. The idea that inspired this book was to describe places with, for once, the complete freedom to be inventive, to express in lyrical terms the sense of being at the very heart of things. The writer's words roam across the leaded rooftops, searching for the people who live beneath the crenellated horizon, observing for a moment a satellite dish perhaps, the odd graffitti, or a chimney that attracts the eye with a particularly expressive shape.

In the mind of the poet, there is an enduring dream: striding towards the sky in a single imaginative step, surrounded by something less tangible than air. Paul Claudel said that for the flight of a single butterfly, the entire sky is needed.

In this world where everything is measured and subjected to judgement, there is still a freer space into which we can all make our escape, be it with our eyes or, for those who dare, with our feet: the roofs, the roofs!

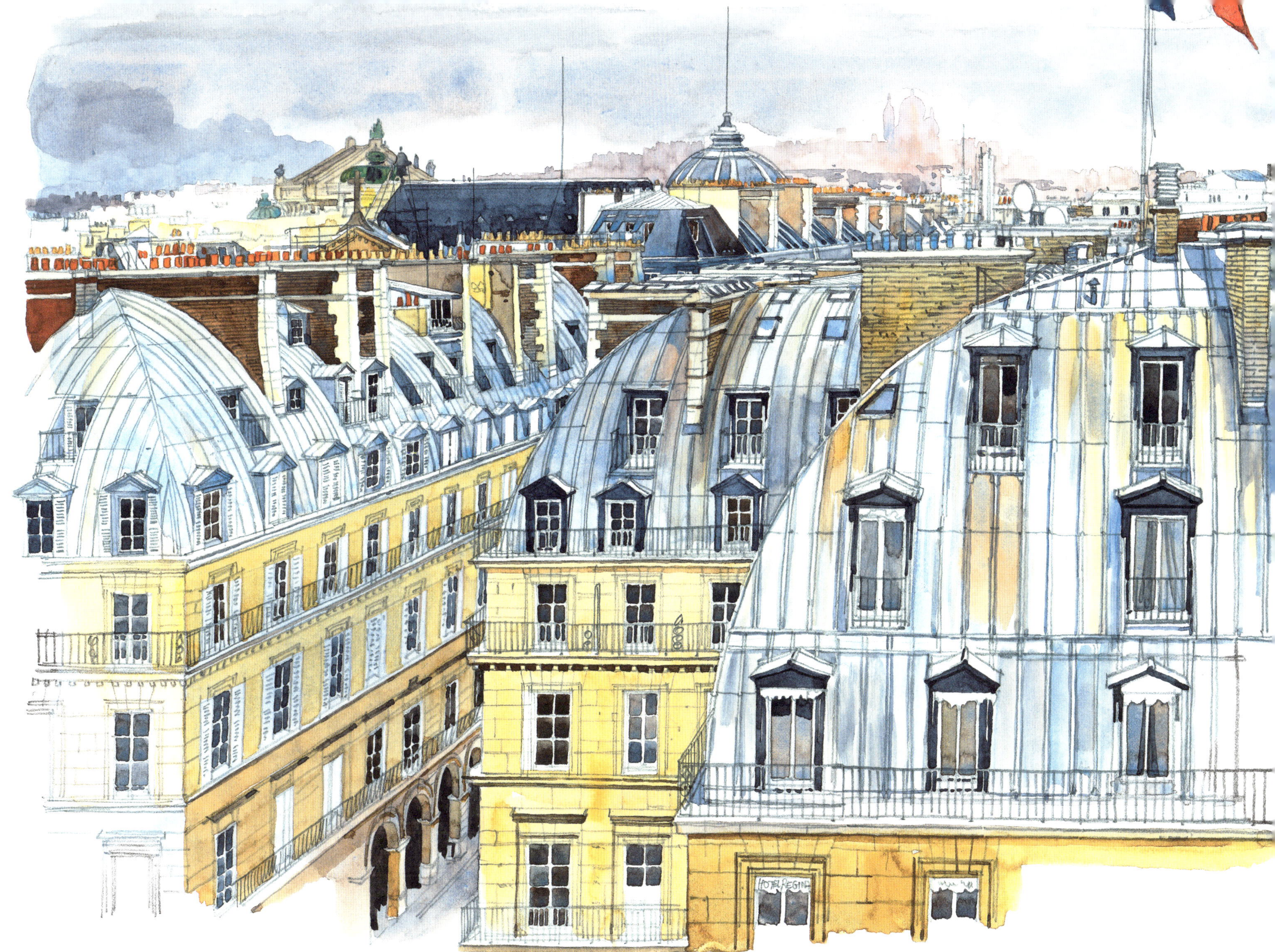

The Opéra – Garnier,
The Sacré-Coeur and the
Rue du Louvre seen from
the Musée des Arts Décoratifs,
Palais – Royal.

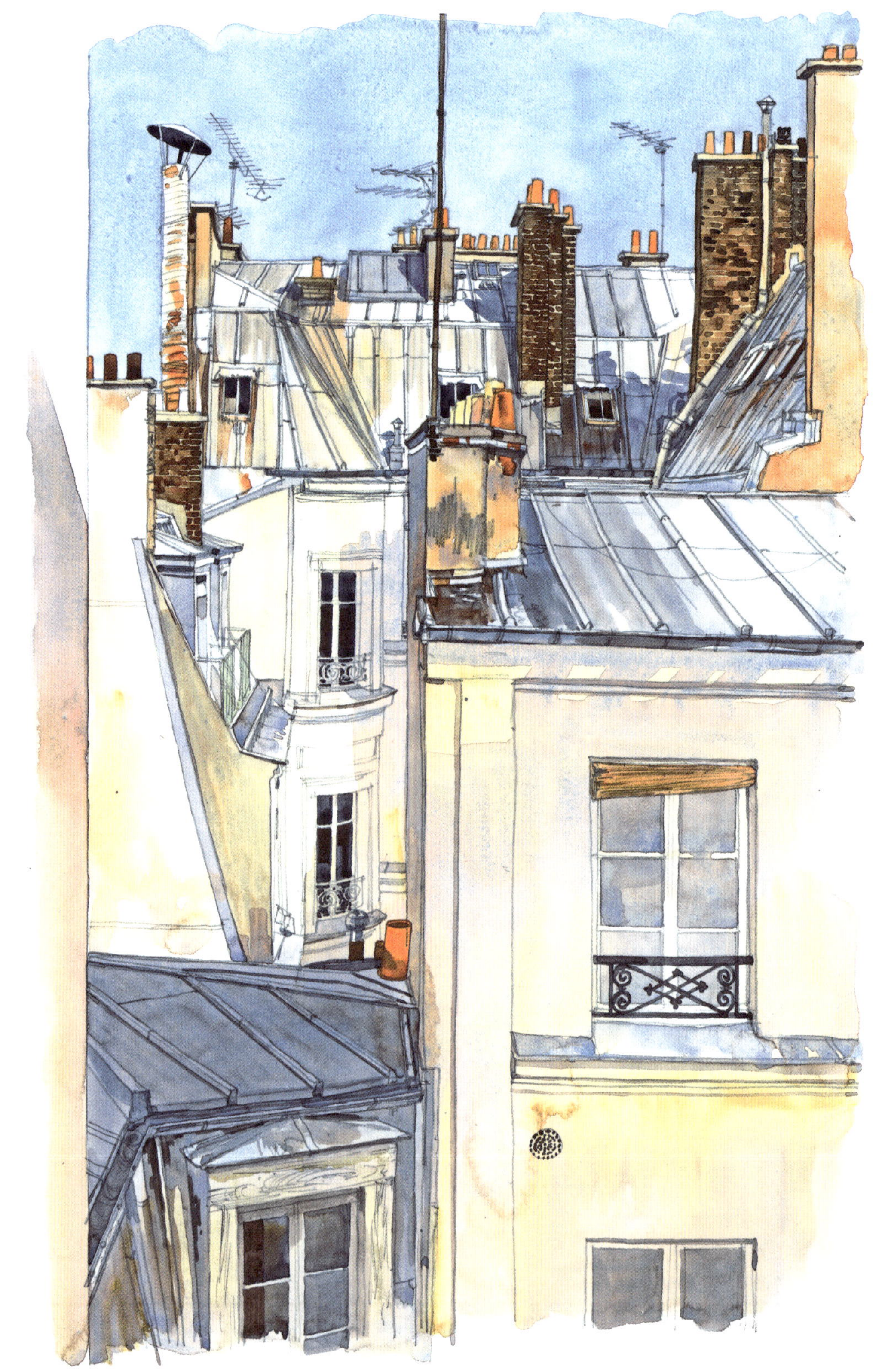

Rue Saint-Denis,
Marais.

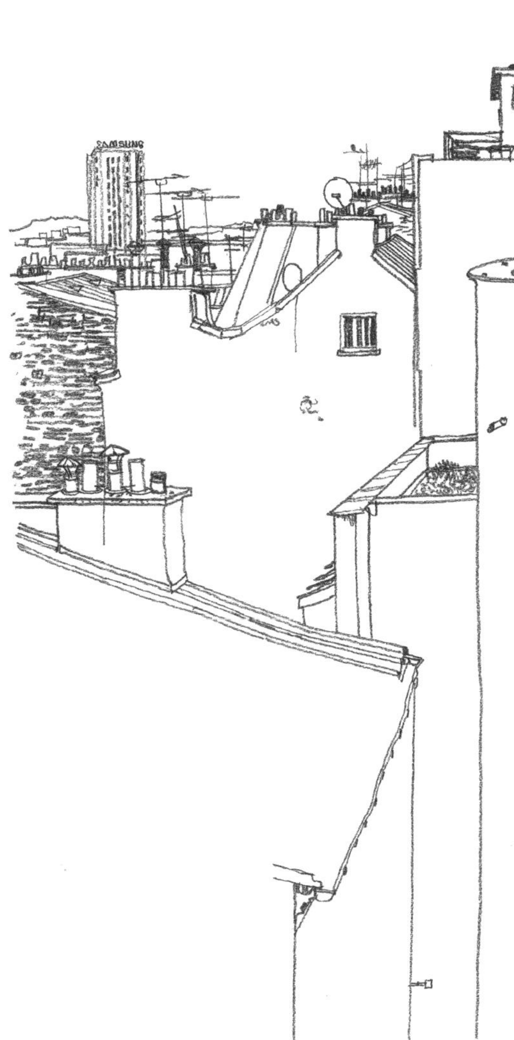

Song of a roof walker

Stranger to himself, he walks against
the sky, improvising the night step after
step, and, on pacing the rooftops, he
compiles these words that whisper to
him in the smoke. He moves through
the air leaving no trace of scent. Only
thoughts thrown against a closed door.

Is he recovering from a love affair, fallen
from high, believing himself eternal, his
finger dipped in beauty's pie, tasted for
the very first time? He leaves for Paris.
Passing rooftops, you should know,
that rivers have been better praised
from down below, than these words
that trace them now, before it rains.

That's what they're worth at the depths
of melancholy, a few footsteps on
footsteps like droplets of rain. Paris does
not exist unless in your mind's eye, you
let this finest of lights, a golden ray, shine
forth amid gentler lights in the streets
and on the rooftops paint a headier grey.

Skimming the rooftops

Only our eyes can follow the effects created by light. As the sun begins to follow its course, shadows waltz across the roofs. Everything our senses take in is a dance in which light and shade play off each other. As the light grows stronger the façades begin to emerge more clearly, overlapping, interlocking forms, planes of lead and, in the distance, delicate stairways of slate. At one moment the roofscape seems to be within reach, then it recedes to a distance. Lazily, indistinctly – that is how the mist speaks on the rooftops of Paris this morning. Dawn has arrived, unannounced. Another autumn begins. It always seems like the first one for lovers opening windows onto the Rue d'Arcole, but it's the last for the red and orange leaves about to invade these gardens. That is how the mist speaks in the City of Light, recounting the seasons. Lazily, indistinctly.

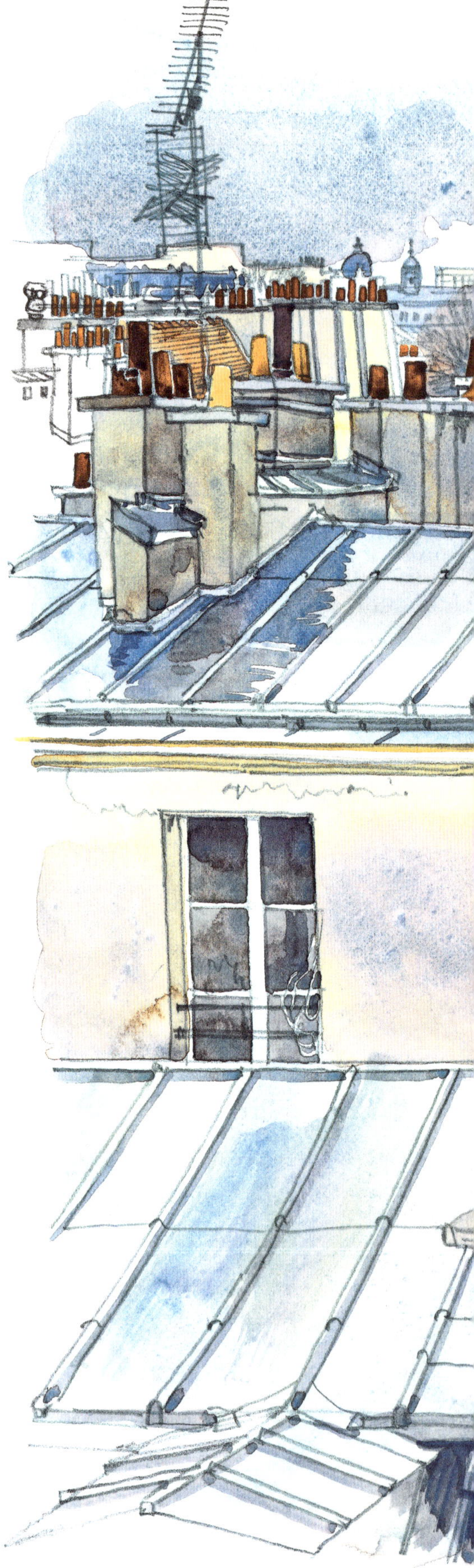

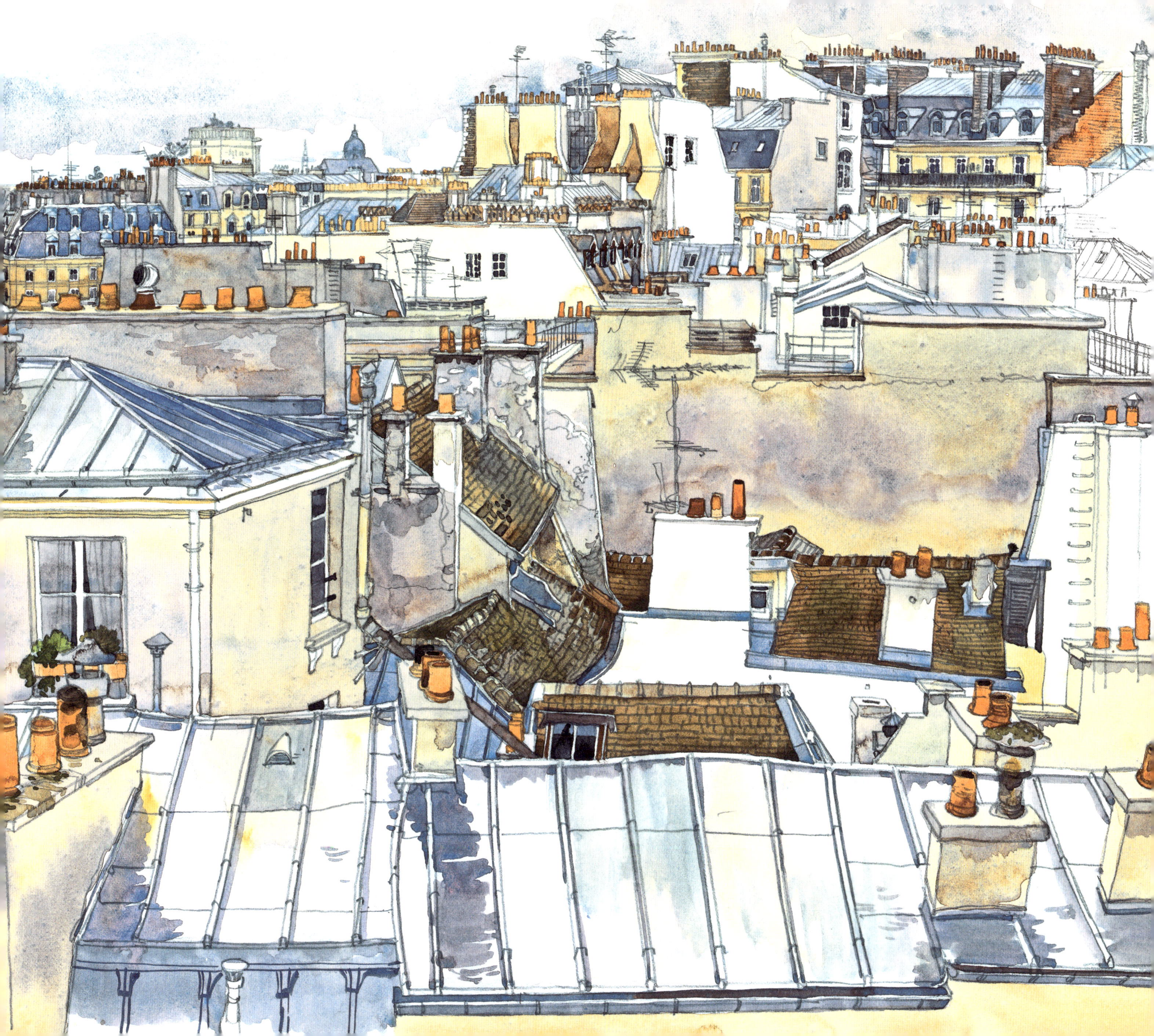

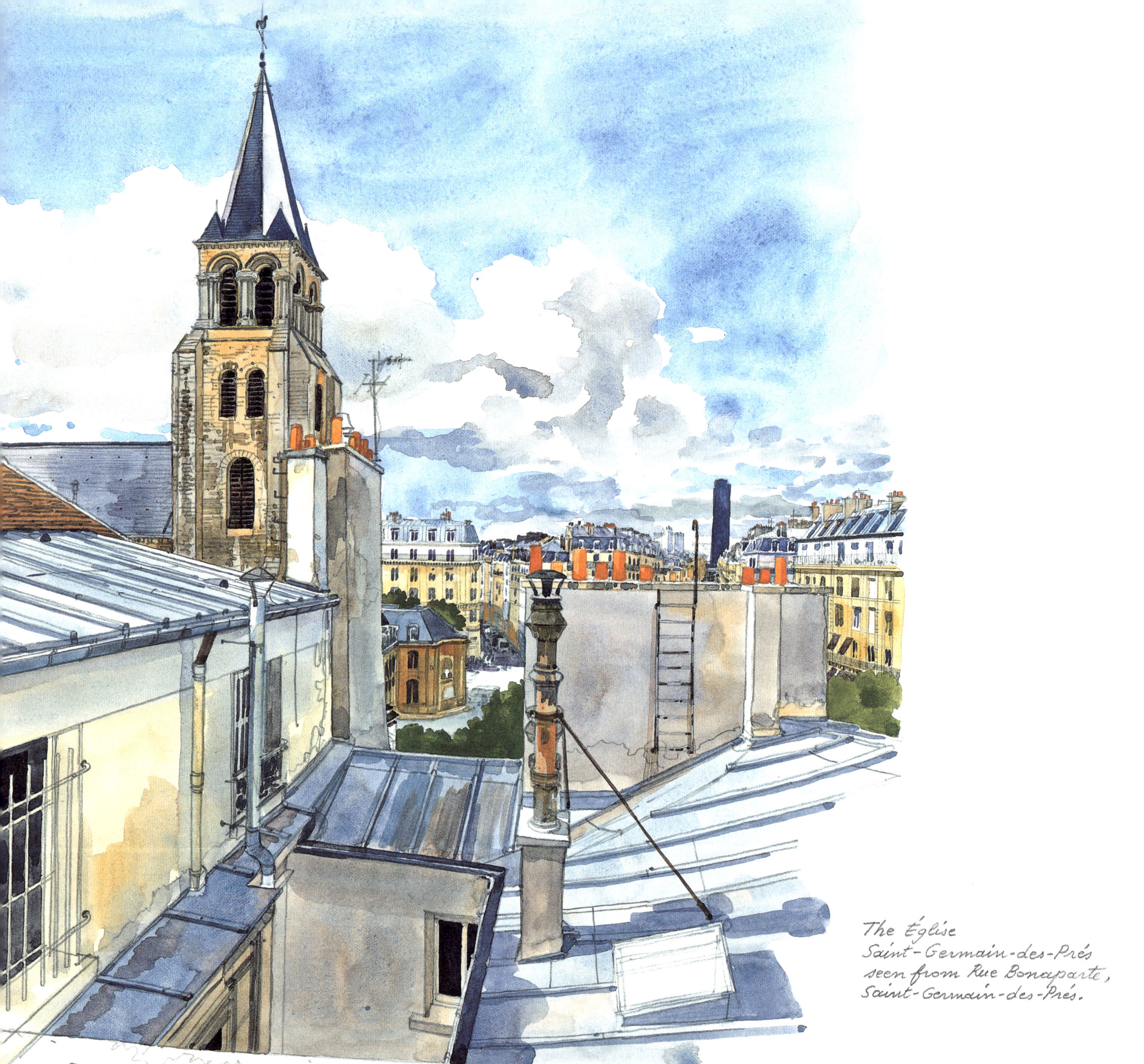

The Église
Saint-Germain-des-Prés
seen from Rue Bonaparte,
Saint-Germain-des-Prés.

Literature viewed from above

She lays her hands on the table. They move by themselves, seizing a little space all around. A light breeze that might be turned into a sentence could be captured with ease here through the mechanism of her fingers. But the idea does not come. The woman sitting on the terrace of the Café de Flore seeks inspiration, her gaze turning first to the boulevard, then towards the church of Saint-Germain, and then up beyond the top of the building façades. "Oh yes, how beautiful it would be," she exclaims to herself, "literature viewed from above!"

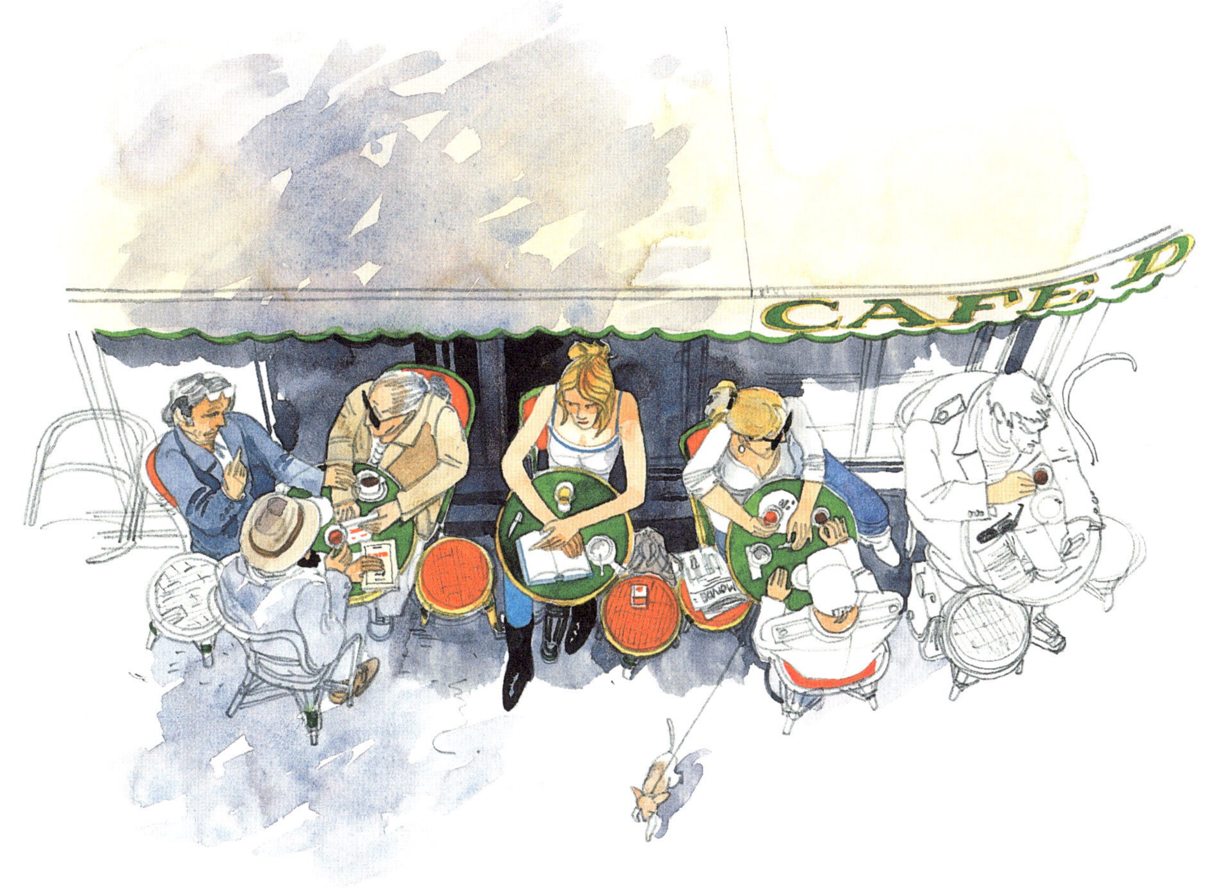

Alcohol, tea and lemonade

Far from the Pont Mirabeau, eighteen metres above the Boulevard Saint-Germain, that is where Guillaume Apollinaire spent his days, in search of his passport to the muses. He had a pigeon loft built, named it the 'poets' perch' and had parties there, where he served alcohol and lemonade. To see his smile, friends and the merely curious had to climb their way up six flights of a spiral staircase. A small opening in the wall, like a loophole in a fortification, served as password; up would pop Guillaume's head, or that of Pipe the cat. As the door creaked open, the visitor was faced with a helmet pierced with holes, with glass balls and marionettes, with rickety chairs, calligrammes traced in dust and books piled up like beehives. Apollinaire was proud of this private retreat reclaimed from the roofs, which he had fitted up himself and decorated with two Matisse drawings. Picasso would arrive, and everything was laughter and daredevilry. They took a ladder to have tea at the very top of the lead roof, comparing their sense of vertigo, but not their fear of living. The other friend, Rouveyre, held back. He would say that he always found something threatening in the crowd of chimneys, with tops like helmets, which surrounded chez Guillaume.

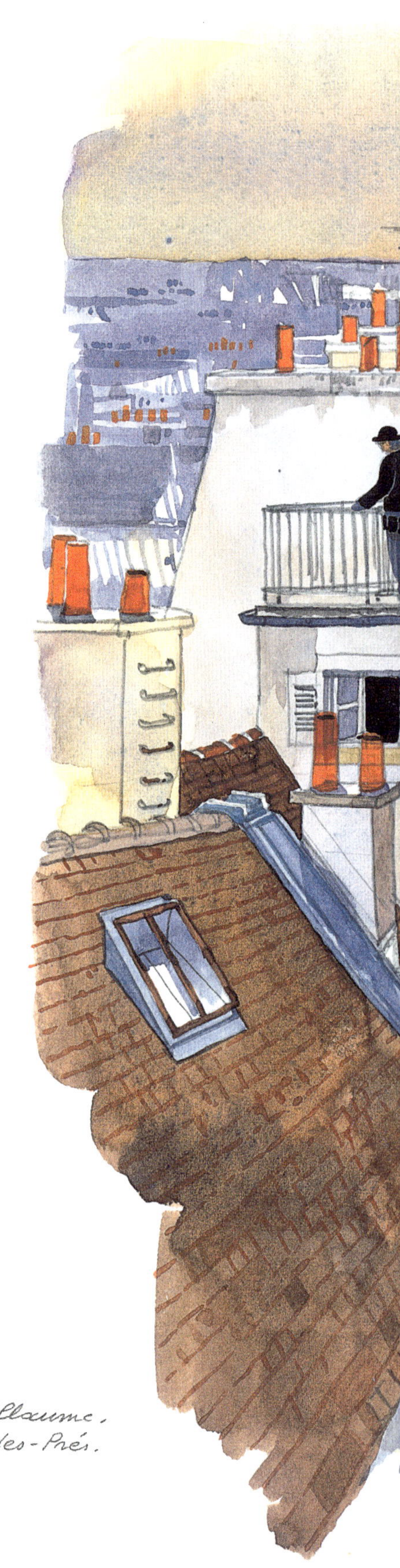

Rue Saint-Guillaume,
Saint-Germain-des-Prés.

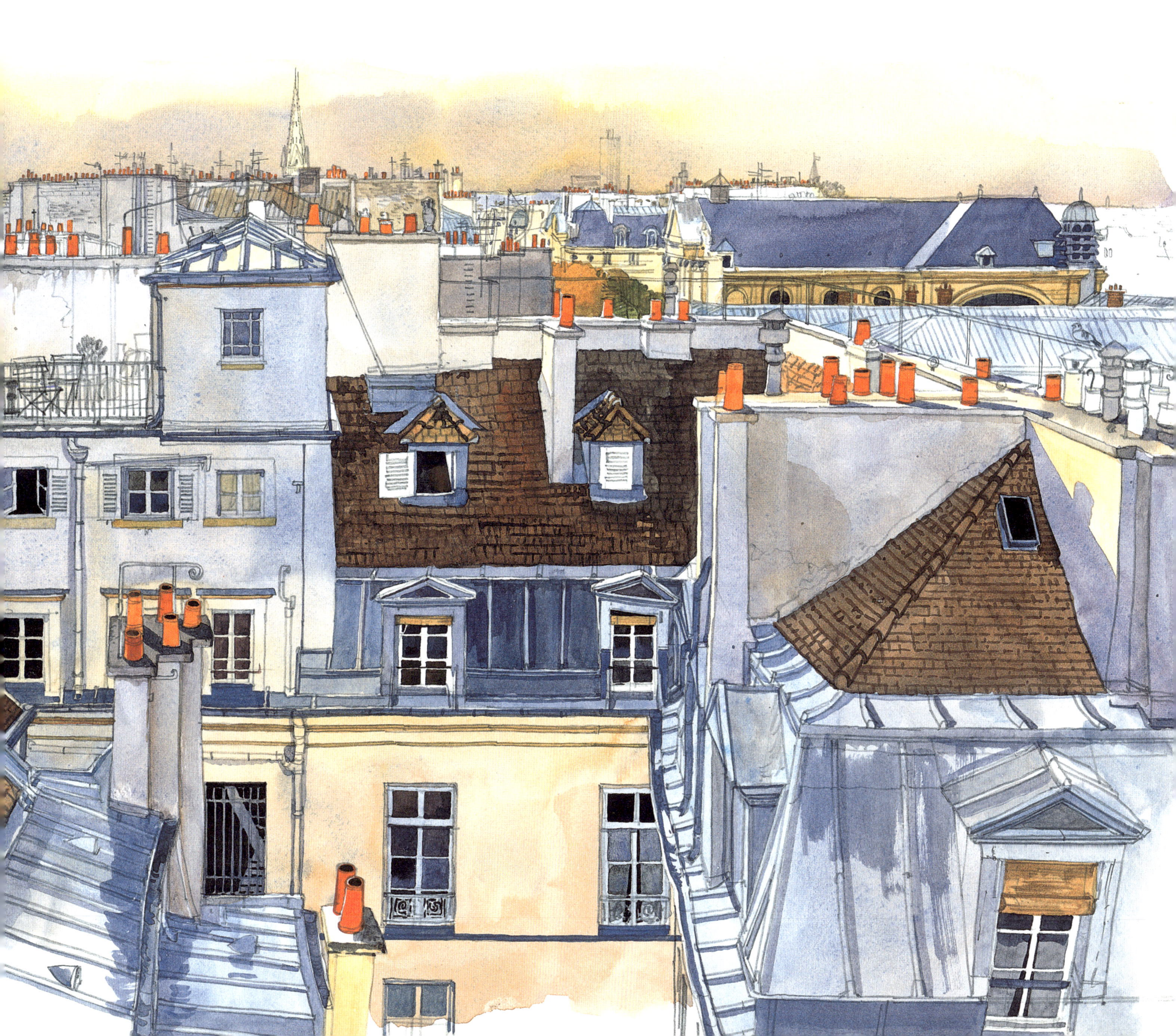

Patina of the night

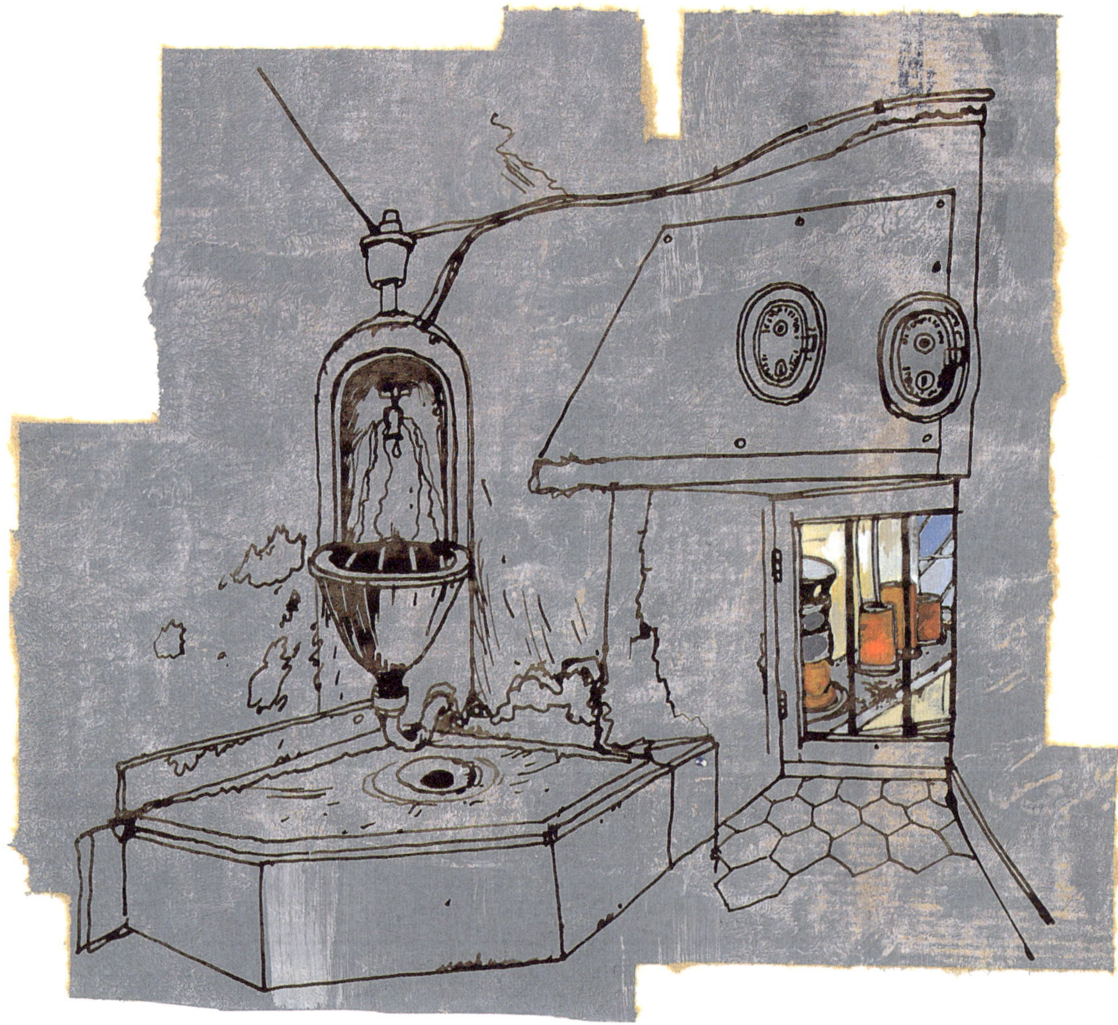

Patina of the night, the sound of water in a pipe, dawn always coming too late or too soon. Looking through the shutters, you arrange in your mind your dreams, the façades far above the pavements, the roofs shrouded in fog, seeming to sway sometimes almost like skirts. It's time to get up. The houses are up already. In Paris, they seem never to have been asleep. Patina of the night, a laugh on the stairway – and so you force yourself to join the hordes of passers-by, the crowds on the metro, in the bistros, in the narrow streets. Today, the crowd will be beautiful.

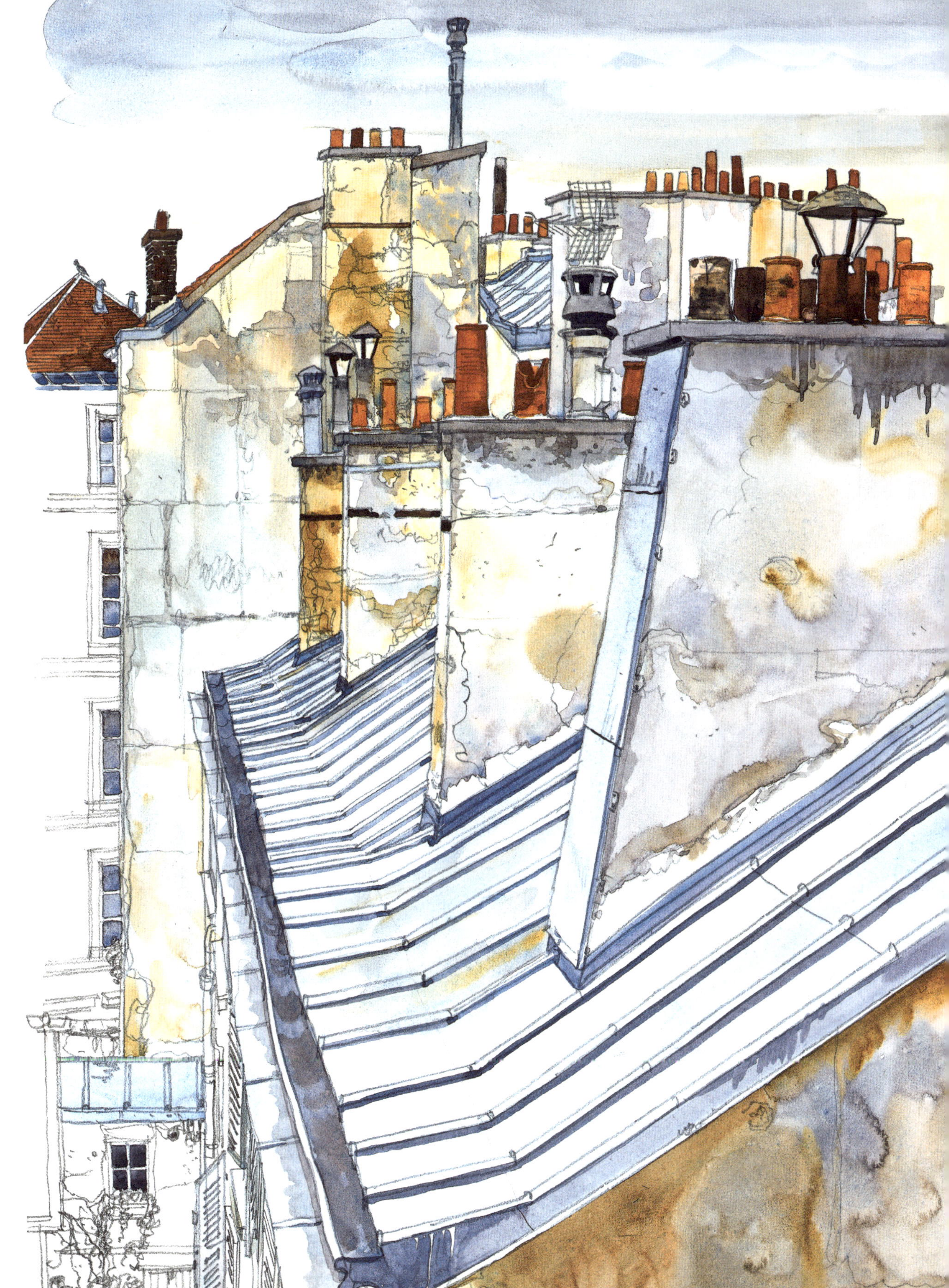

Rue du Parc-Royal.
Marais.

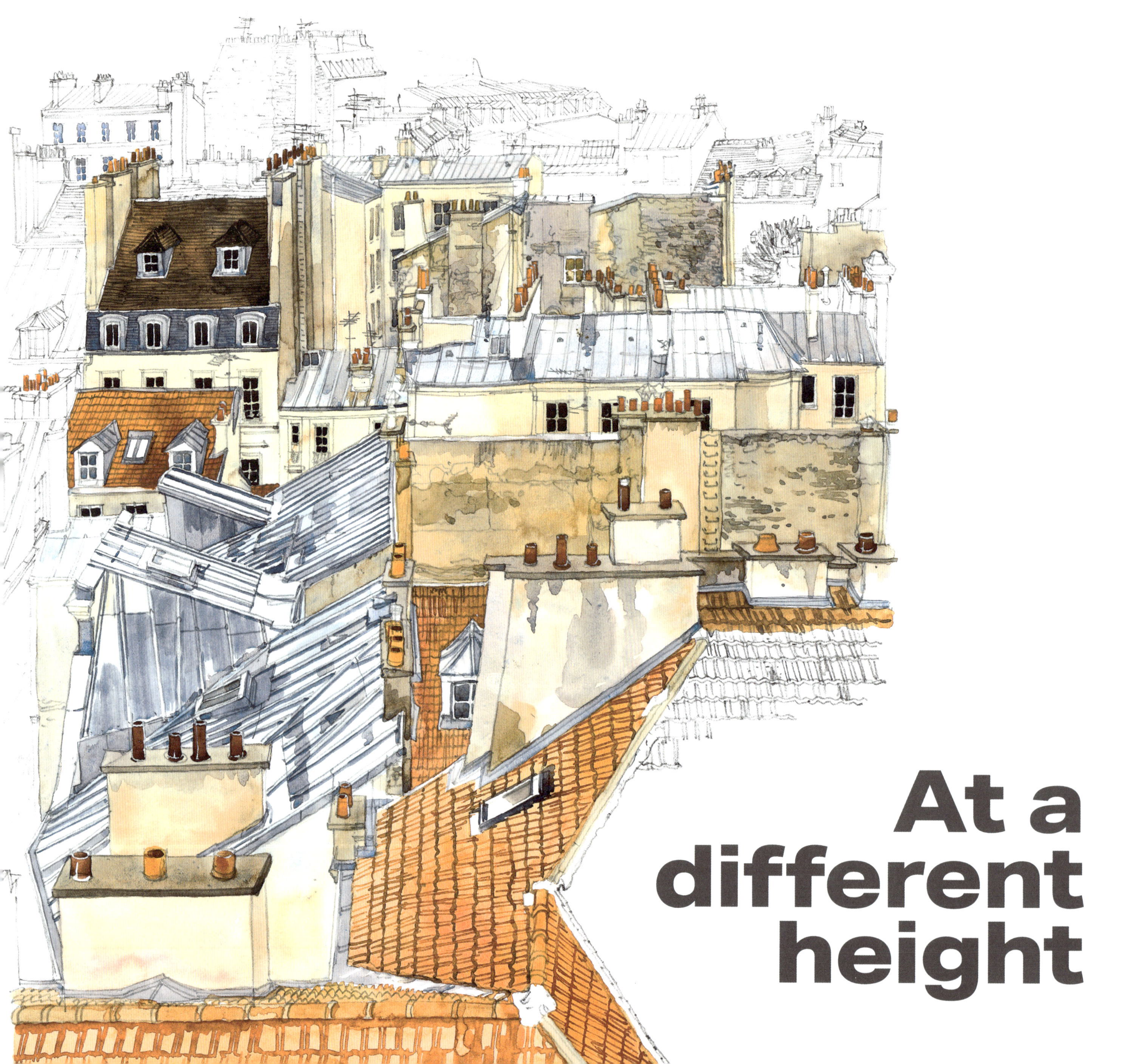
At a
different
height

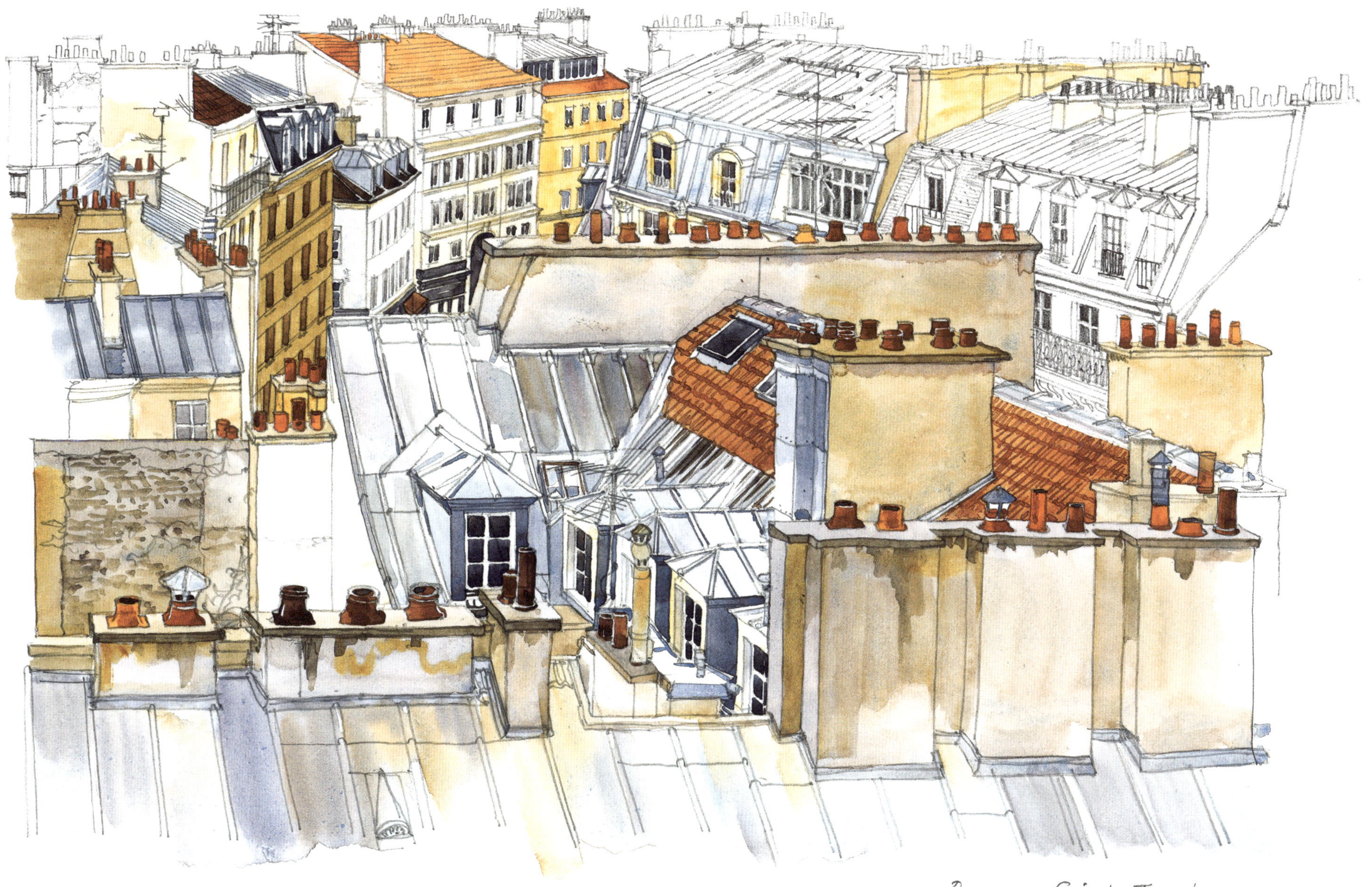

You see life from up on the rooftops, there's no shade up here. The sky comes right down as if to eat out of your hand. You look at Paris as if through a long zoom lens, with its streets and alleys raised up or enclosed, running through the morning like wet furrows. You're aware of the sound of voices beneath these roofs and, at this moment, even against the noise of the city, now almost a continuous drone, you seem to hear them all. Paris shows her rooftops to those who will see them. In your mind's eye, a few pictures come to life, a bright reflection, a strand of sheer beauty, that immediately spark off other images. And suddenly, Paris is there in front of you, in all its magic, at an unfamiliar altitude.

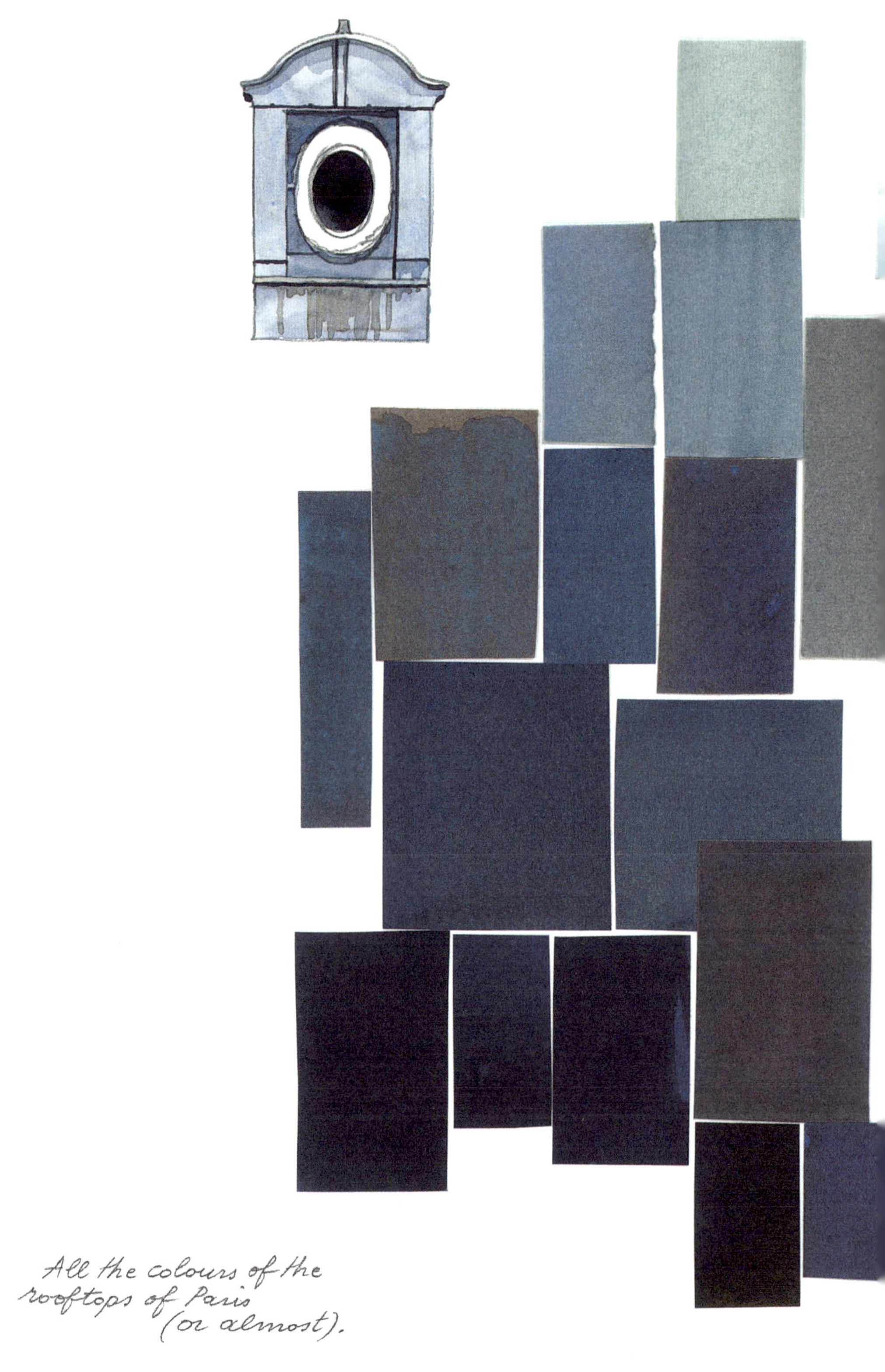

All the colours of the
rooftops of Paris
(or almost).

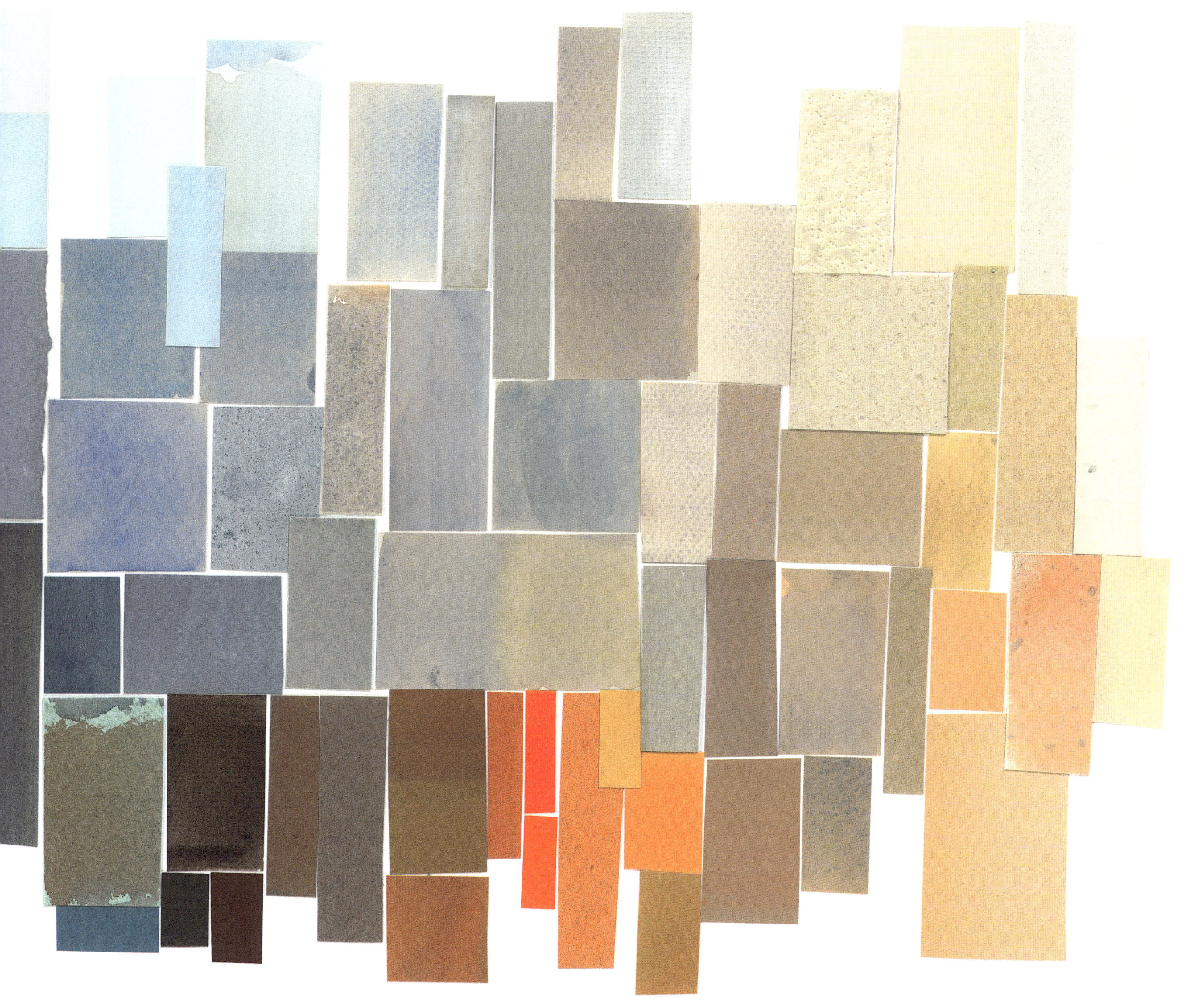

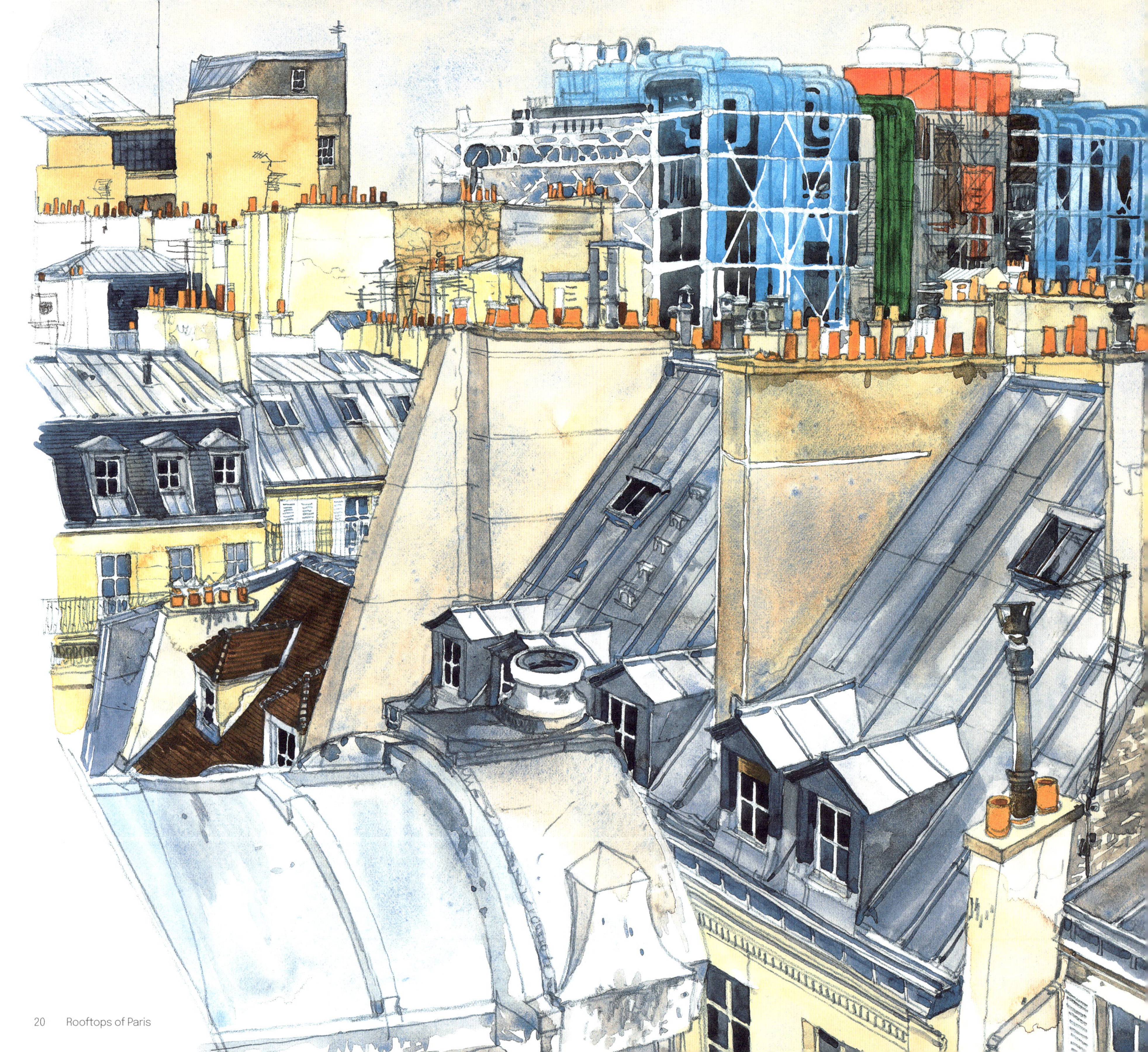

In praise of grey

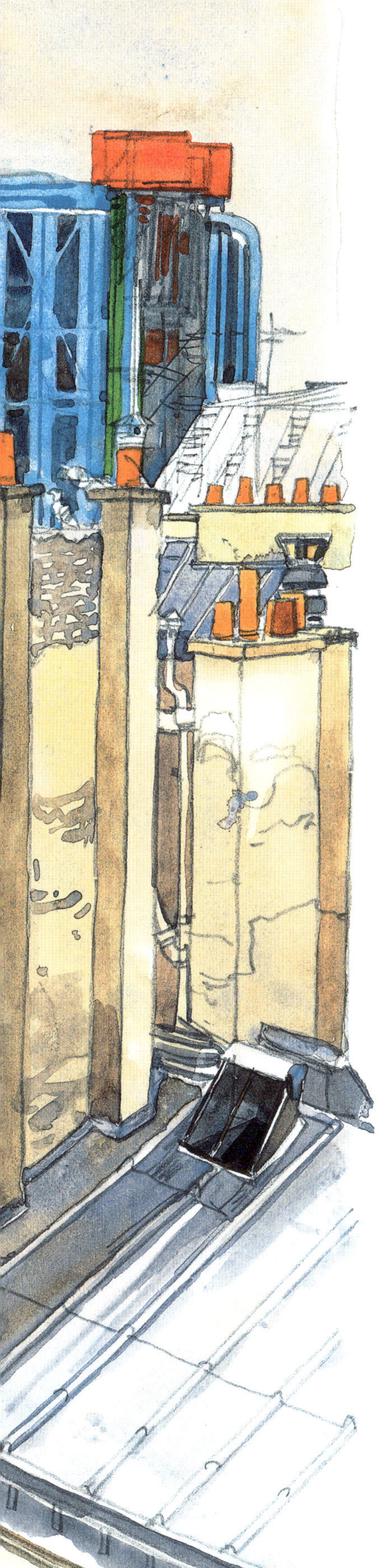

At this modest altitude, it's time to speak out for grey, so often criticised for being monochrome, as if responsible for the greyness of peoples' spirits. What other colour has such subtle nuances? The roofs of Paris stand as unimpeachable witnesses, wherever they perch or lean. Sometimes greyish blues face the sky, verging on beige; at other times, a touch of mauve-grey finds its way onto the upper reaches of the façades. And then the spectrum broadens, starting with the range of ochres, then that grey almost the colour of light clay, and the shadowy off-white caused by the passage of time, spreading across the rooftops as if to cover them with cloth. There isn't the slightest melancholy in grey. When the watercolourist lays a neutral grey, the first drop of terracotta to fall on it warms it up: a metamorphosis takes place from grey into a rooftop kingdom, a mysterious shadow-filled space or a mirror to reflect the merest dancing cloud. And in the distance run the blue and red pipes of what looks like a big ship. This afternoon, that particular roof looks as if it has been dusted with flour, turning grey in the light. Perhaps, soon, even the Centre Pompidou itself will melt into its surroundings as part of this universal eulogy to grey.

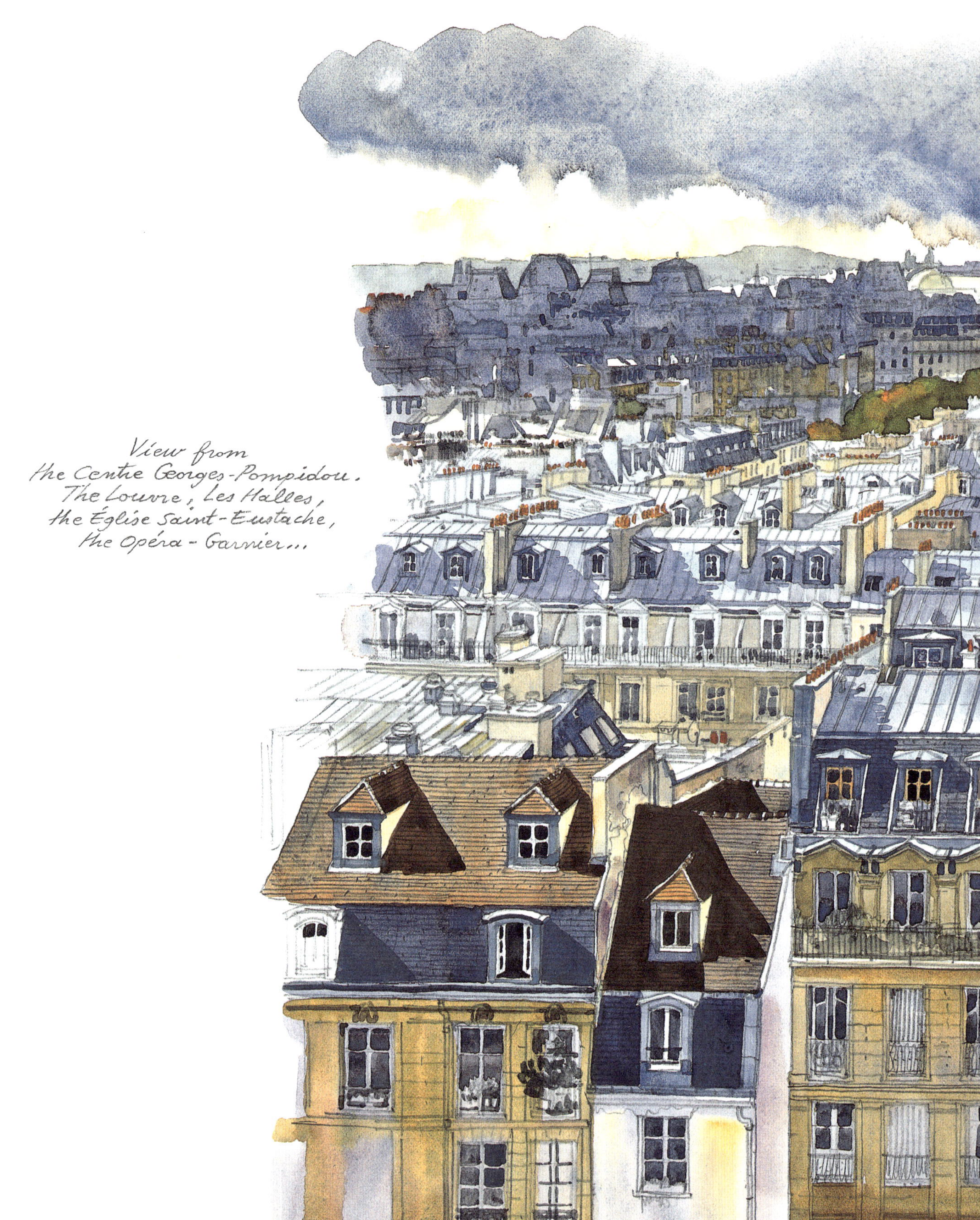

View from
the Centre Georges-Pompidou.
The Louvre, Les Halles,
the Église Saint-Eustache,
the Opéra-Garnier...

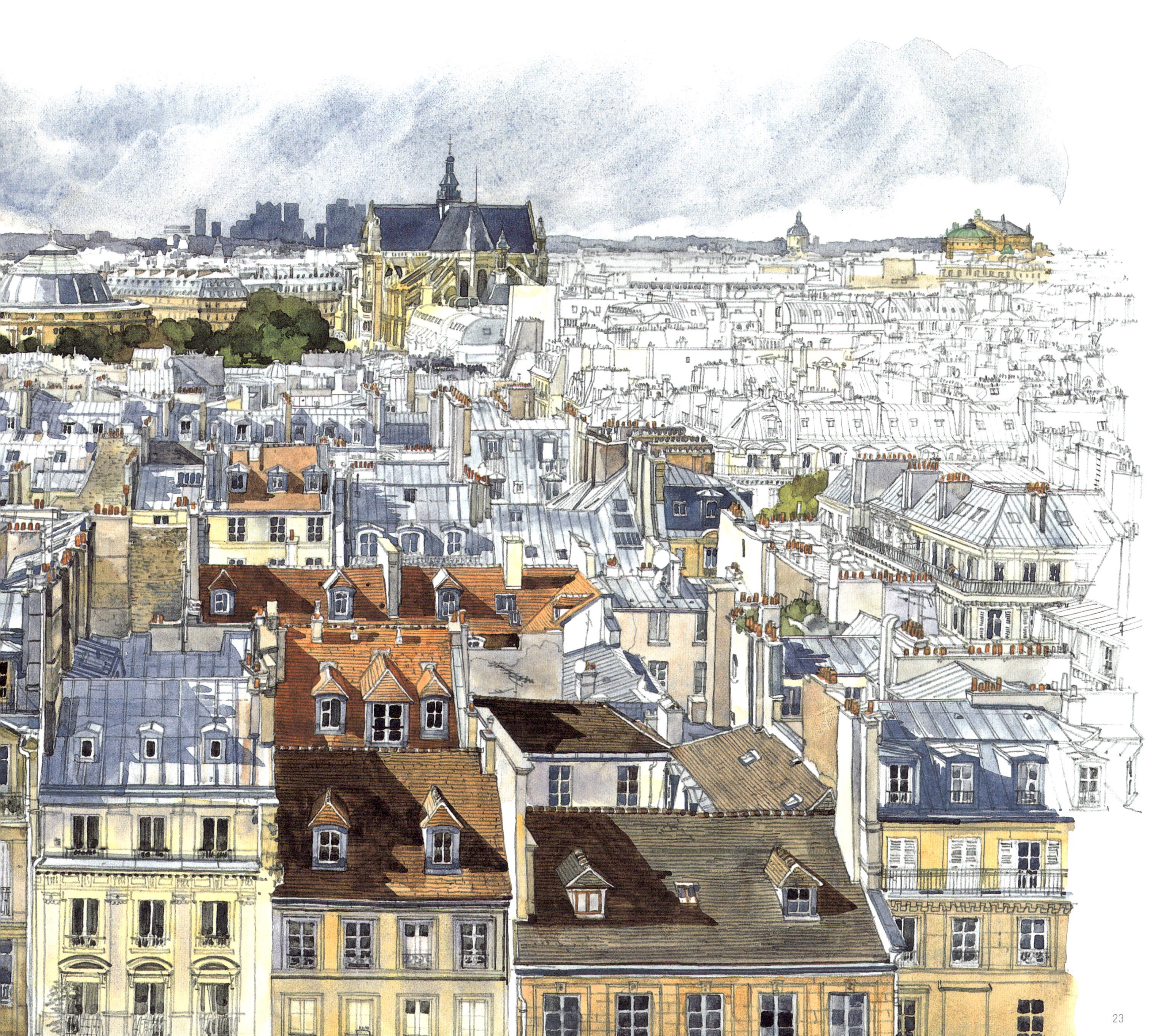

A colourful people

In Paris, there's a hidden people whose diverse, motley families happily rub along together. A people who speak during both day and night, and are always there, on rooftops, above façades and squares, in the sky or down in the street. Who are these people? They are colours. In the building shown here in the painting, there lives someone who might be an ethnologist or he might just be a happy madman. At his feet or, rather, before his eyes live the beige people, ecru or chalky-white, depending on their mood; the ochre people, extending to pink when required, the blue people, twirling, running down onto high walls punctuated by warm, orangey-brown chimneys. It's good to leave the land of shapes for the one of people ablaze with colour.

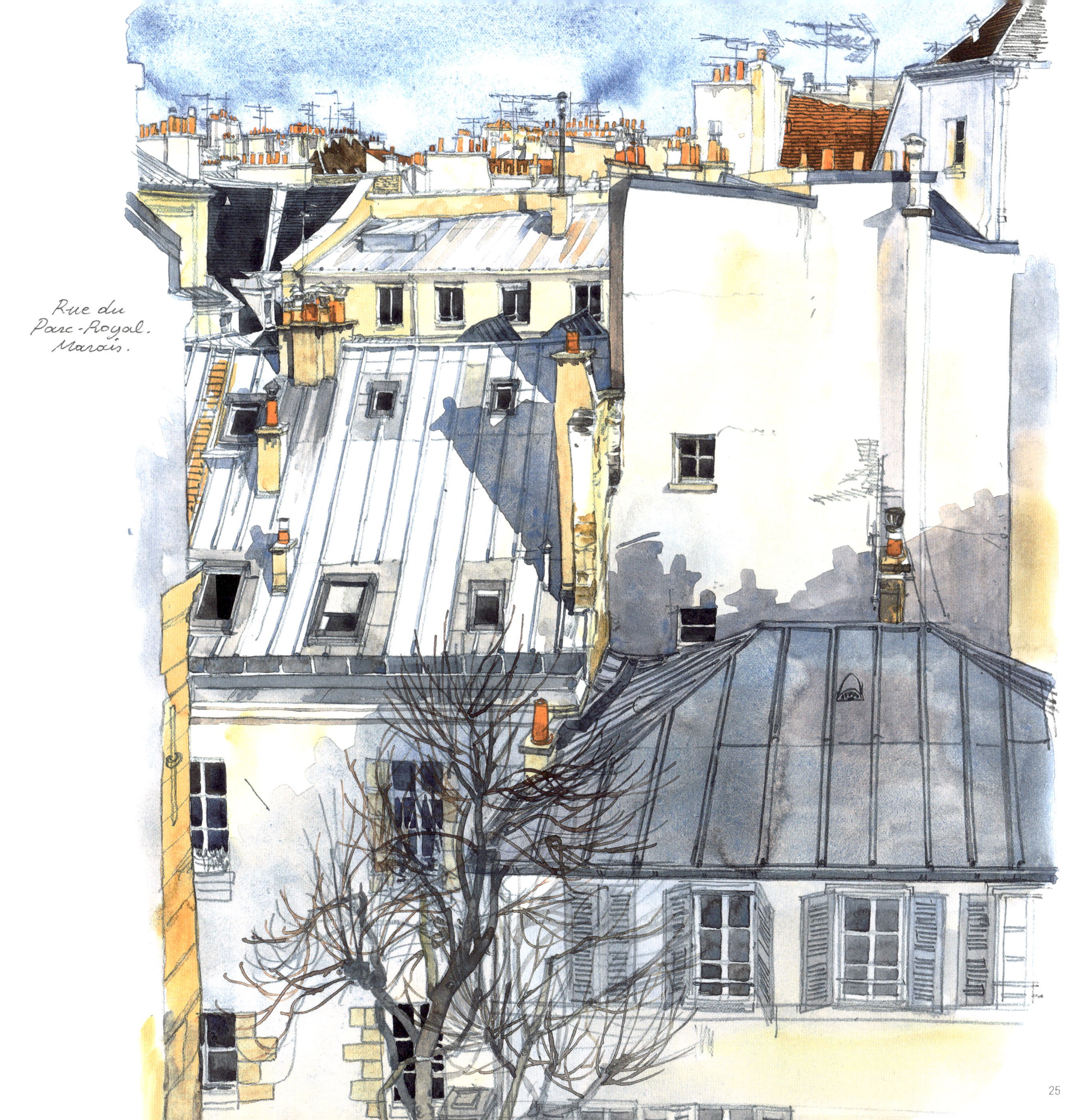

Rue du
Parc-Royal.
Marais.

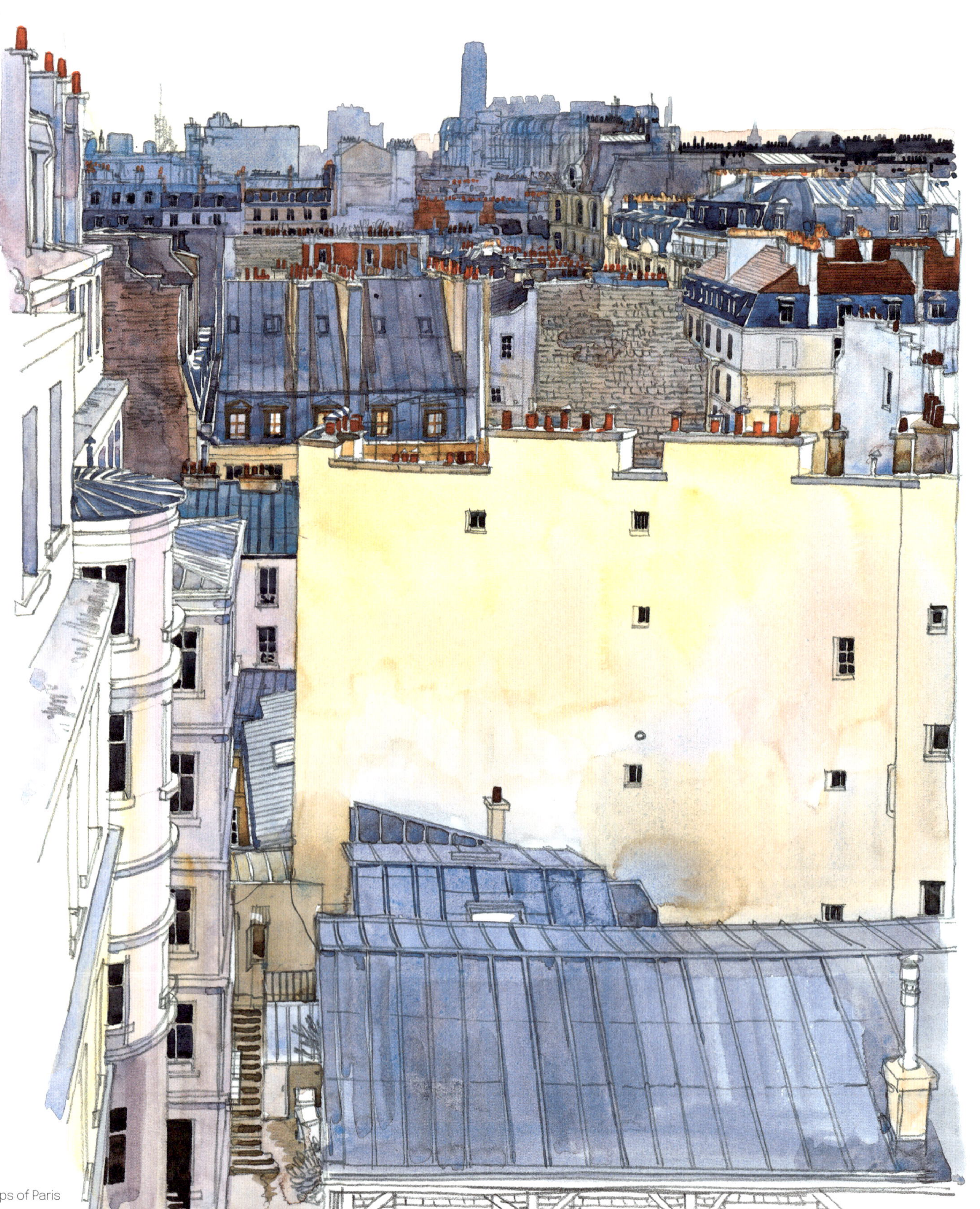

Rue Béranger,
République.

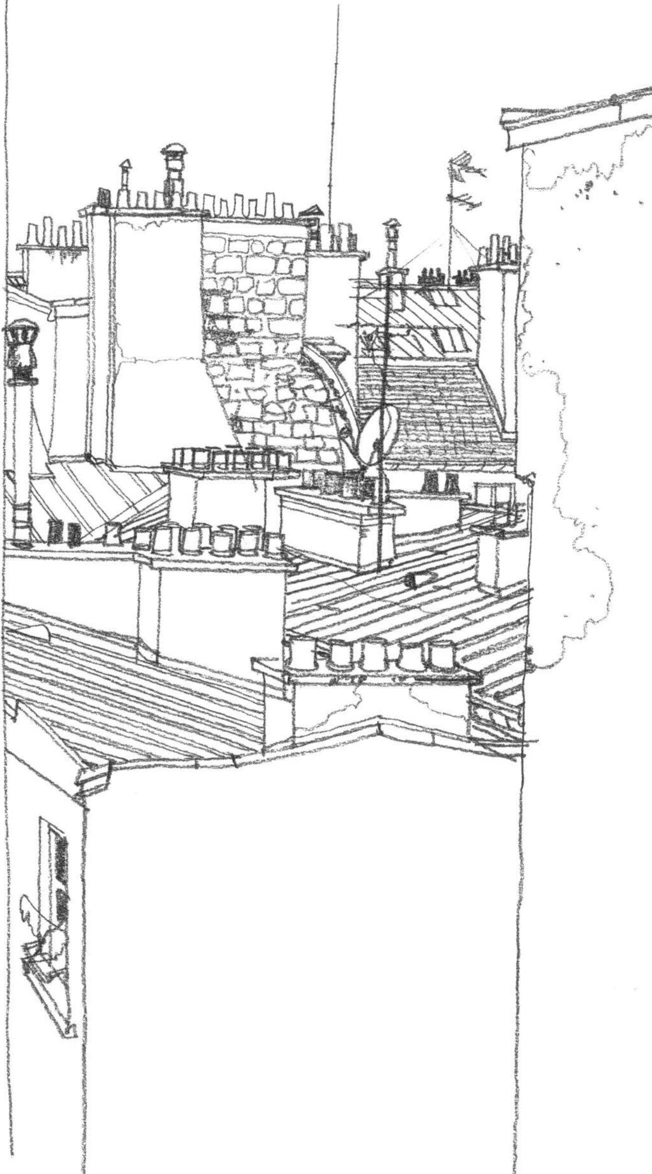

Fortress

On a wall which looks like a fortress, the sun refuses to set. Spreading lazily over the façade, it creates its own desert landscape, revealing all manner of sandy hues. Further away, the shadows have their own realm in the Rue de Bretagne and the Square du Temple, towards Beaubourg. Thanks to a slow parting of the clouds, the fortress is set ablaze, bright and clear as a page on which the time left for each of us simply to while away, or to use gainfully in the contemplation of a single image, can be recorded easily.

Flight to light

The staircase winds its way upwards. There's a lingering smell of old polish and damp. The stairs creak just as they have always done; a sound unchanged since the time of maids' quarters, attics where lives were carried on at a whisper. The view is blocked on the side where the artist imagined a landscape hitherto unconquered, but about to be captured. The painter of roofs is worried. Has he climbed up all this way for nothing? A surprised tenant, a greeting, a garret and a modest ray of sunshine. He's found what he was looking for. The grandeur of Paris can be glimpsed through this new chink, this odd little spyhole. Quick, let's get going. There's just enough time before the light goes. The painter applies a neutral colour, then adds the merest hint of terracotta to his palette. Bit by bit, almost imperceptibly, reds and blues come together in a slow dance of celebration. At the tip of a paintbrush, we enter a land of pure enchantment.

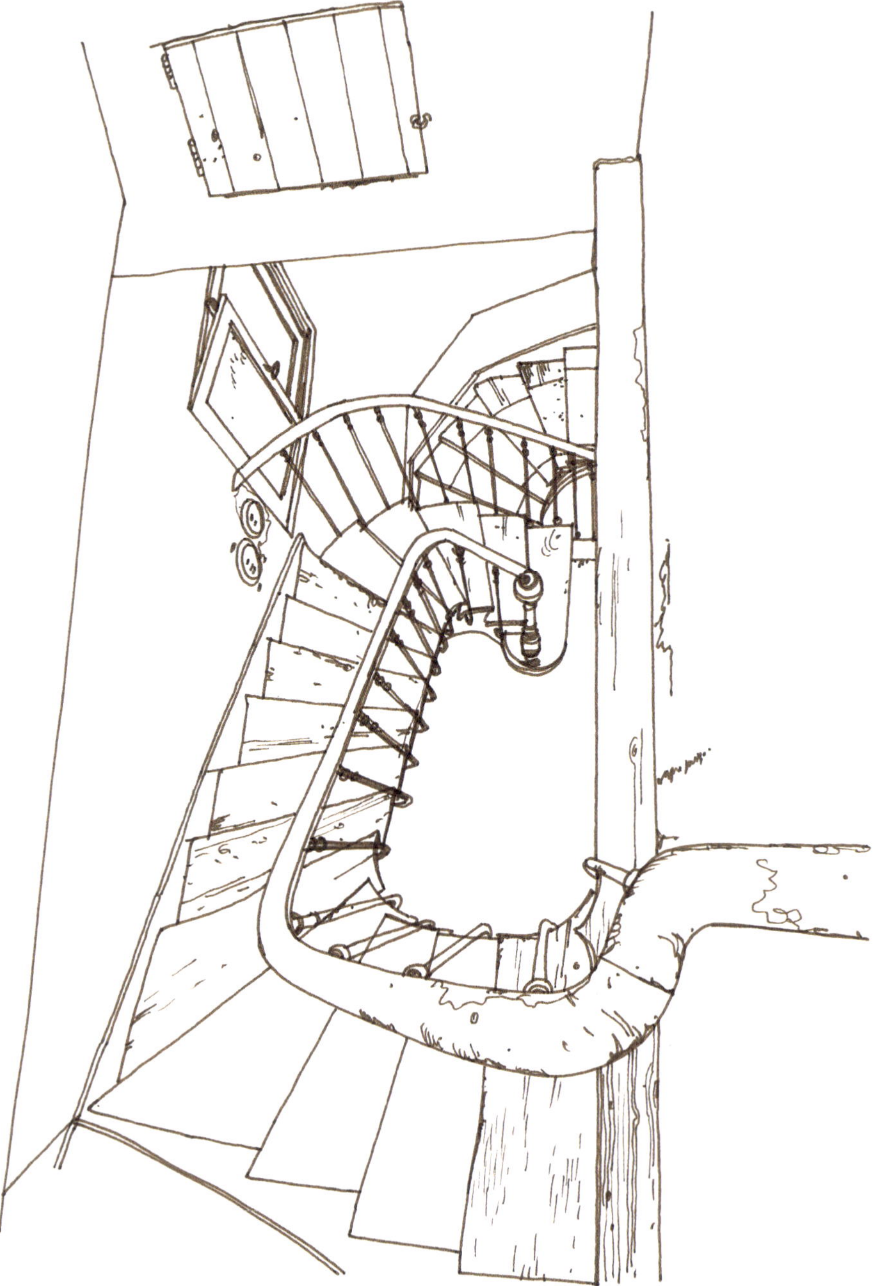

One step closer

Everybody knows about poets in Paris, living in garrets, suffering and penniless. But has anyone considered that under that attic roof the poet was just a little closer to the sky?

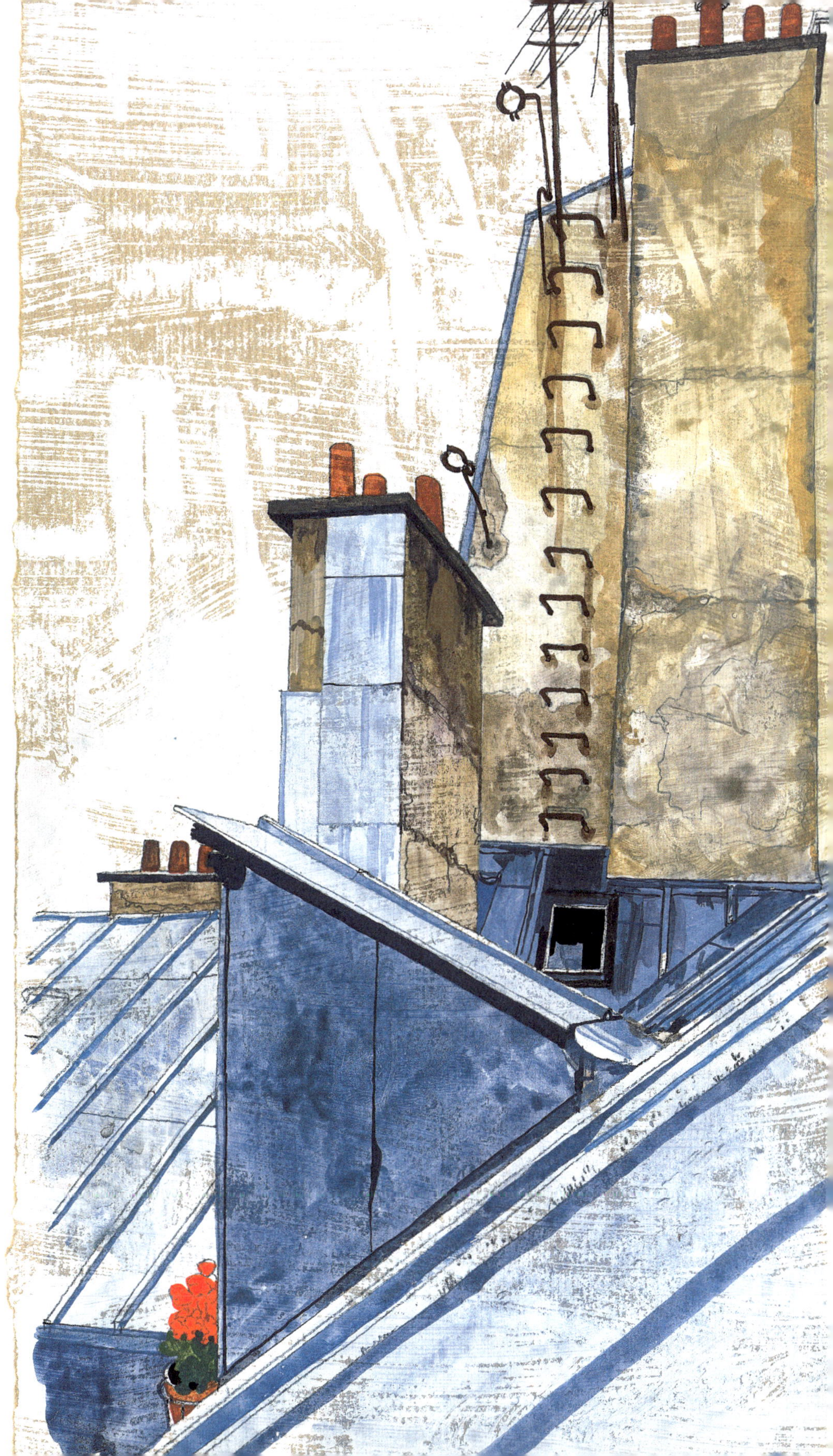

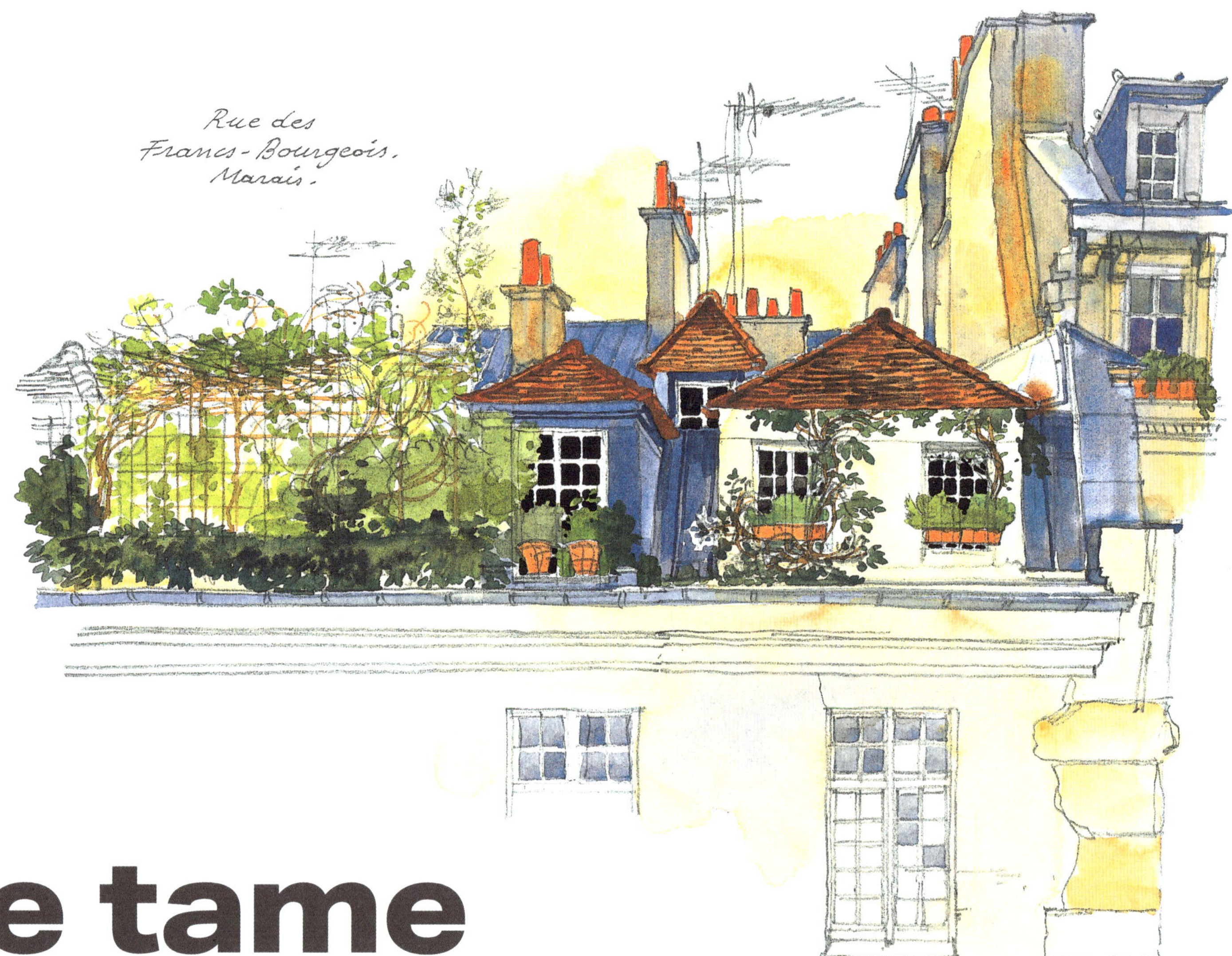

The tame jungle

We're all sparrows at heart, flying over part of the city, over houses huddled closely together as if trying to keep warm, or leaning on each other like unstable rows of dominoes. Suddenly we spy a patch of green. An oasis hanging in the air, flowerpots lined up like targets in a shooting gallery, where, beneath bamboo pergolas, plants colonise space as slowly as a bird building a nest. Geraniums, boxwood, ivy, flashes of colour, little dashes of fragrance, everything competes for supremacy in the deep-set streets or on the façades of aristocratic houses in the Marais. We're all sparrows at heart, especially when we spot the growing tendril of a creeping plant or, perhaps in our imagination, a secret corner where a tempting blackberry or a hidden raspberry trembles on its stem.

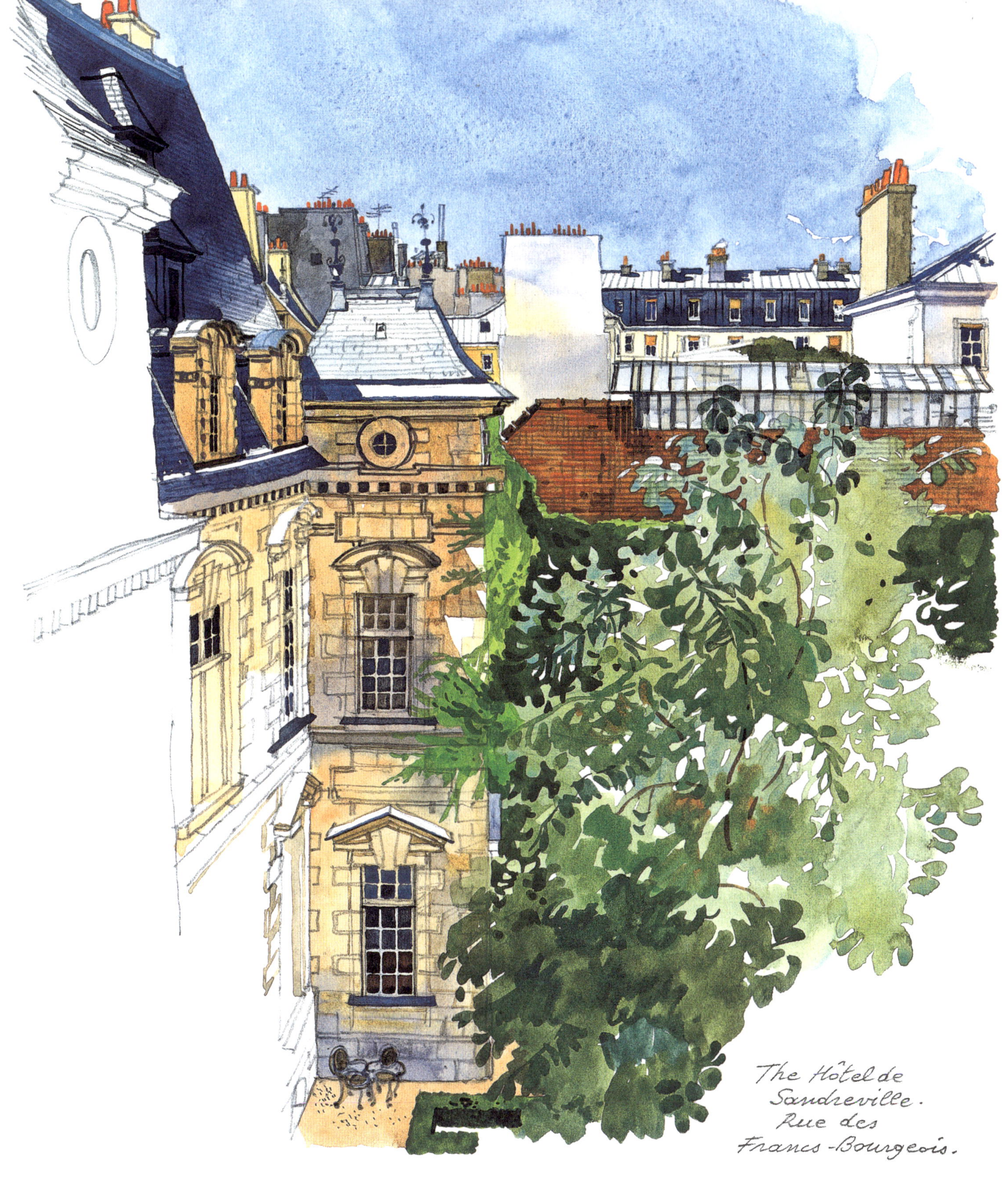

The Hôtel de
Sandreville.
Rue des
Francs-Bourgeois.

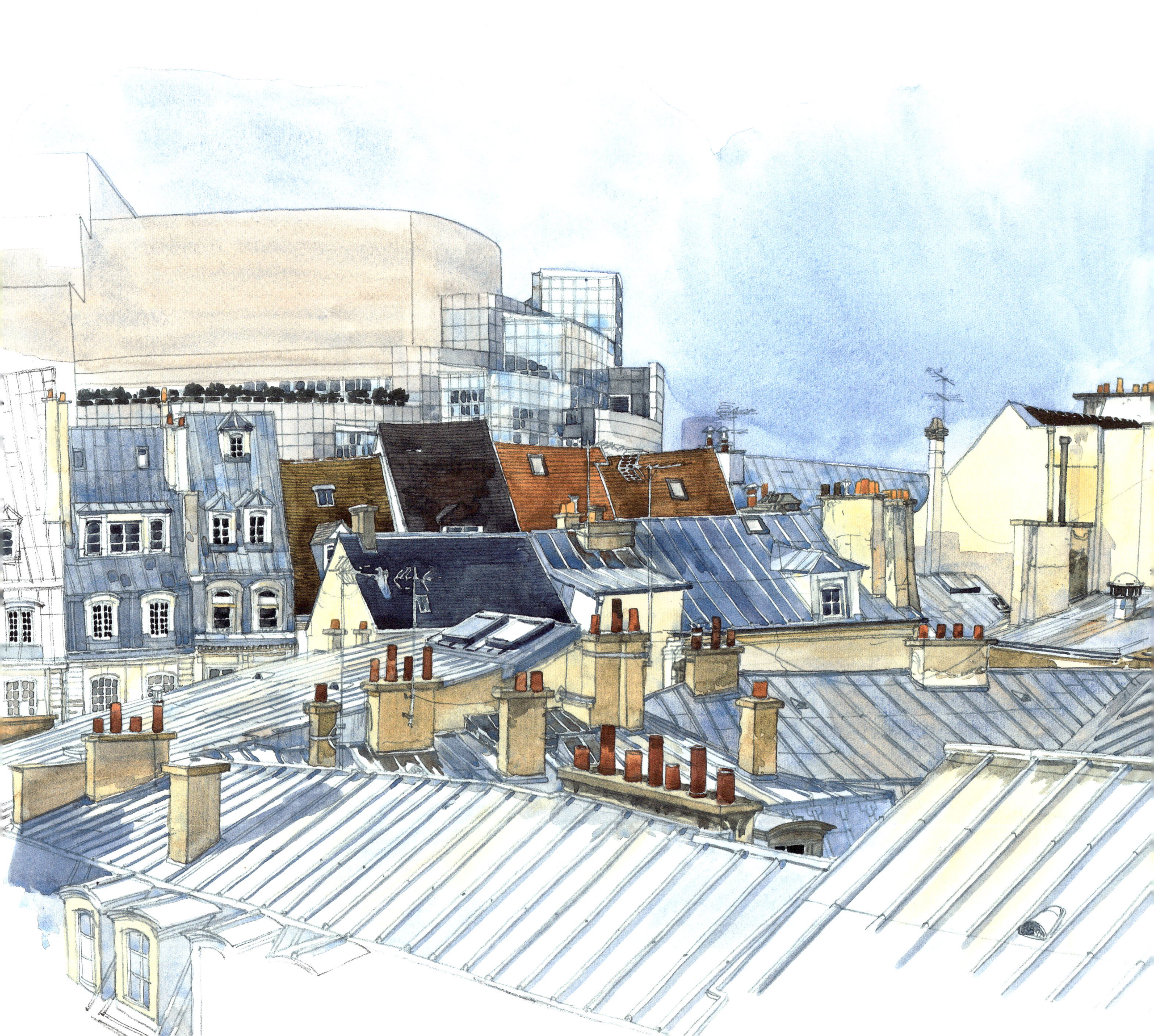

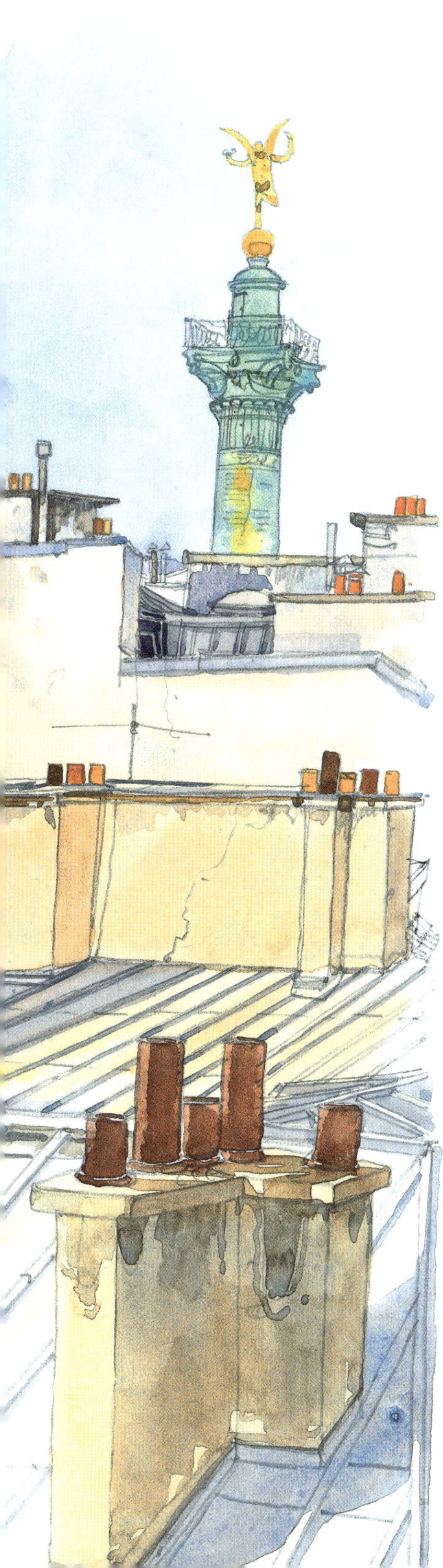

To the Génie de la Bastille

Here is the unfallen angel, wingéd and richly clad in gold, claiming no golden parachute.

The Opéra-Bastille and the Colonne de Juillet seen from the Passage du Cheval-Blanc. Bastille.

Chimney piece

Two roofers are busy at work. A broken chimney pot no doubt. Behind them is the Colonne Vendôme, as indifferent to their presence as to those who came before them. It was brought down at the time of the Commune, then raised again like a slender lighthouse. The men repair stonework, while looking down on the square, where chauffeurs wait in front of shop windows, brushing the dust off their vehicles. Children's voices rise up from the Rue Saint-Honoré. The city is at times humming, at times seeming to pause for reflection. A limousine starts up. The chimney pot is back in place and the world moves on.

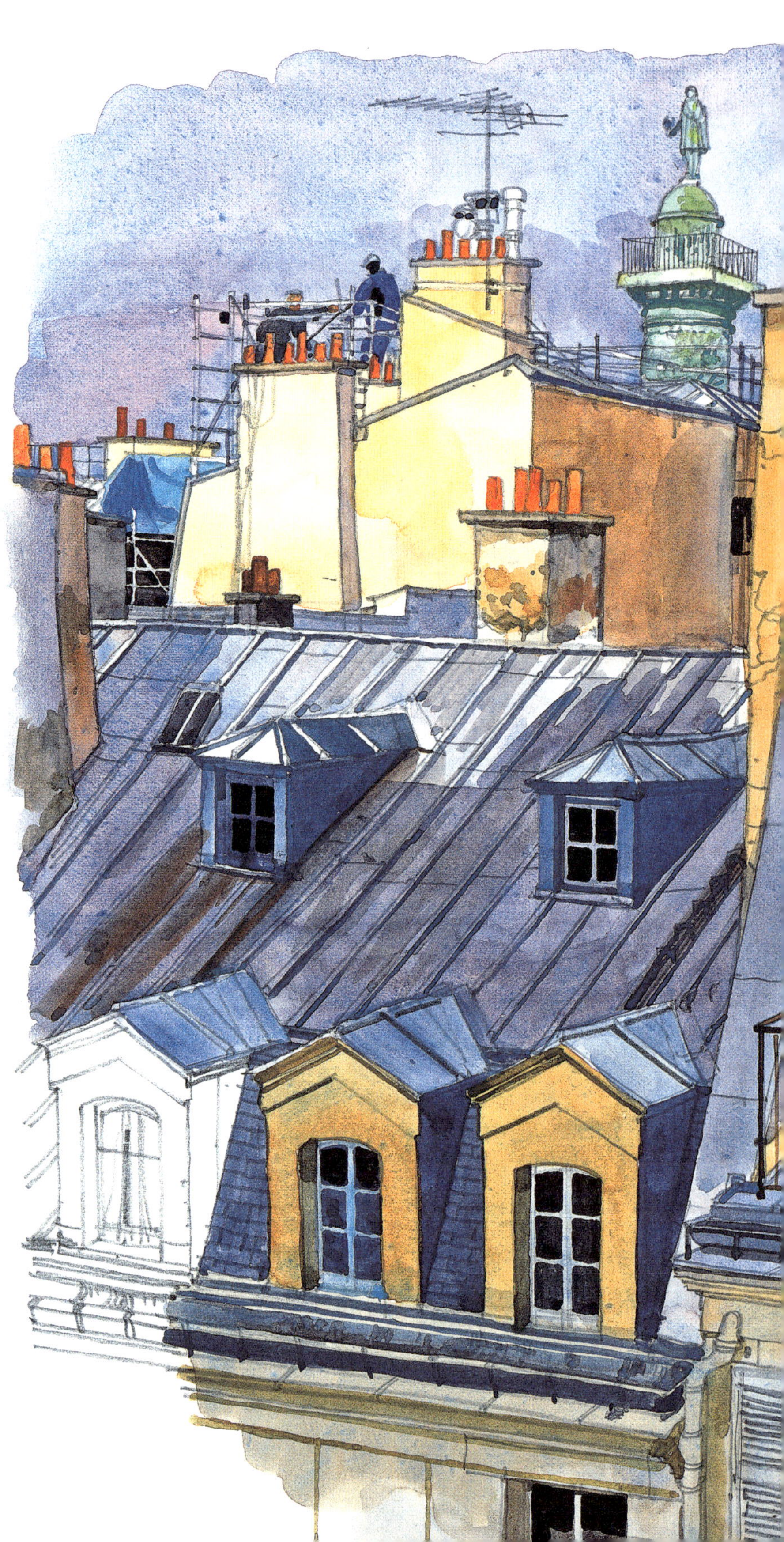

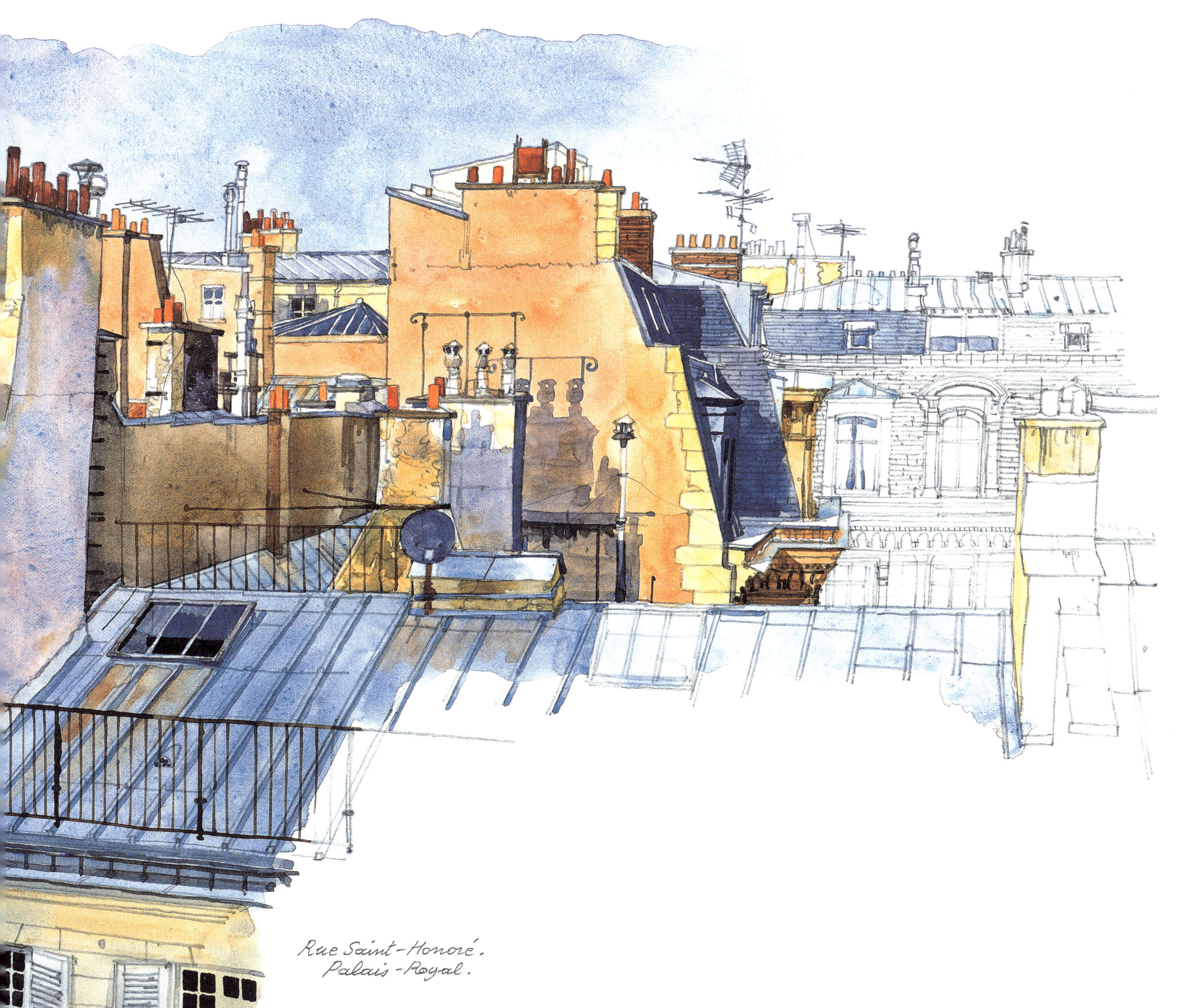
Rue Saint-Honoré.
Palais-Royal.

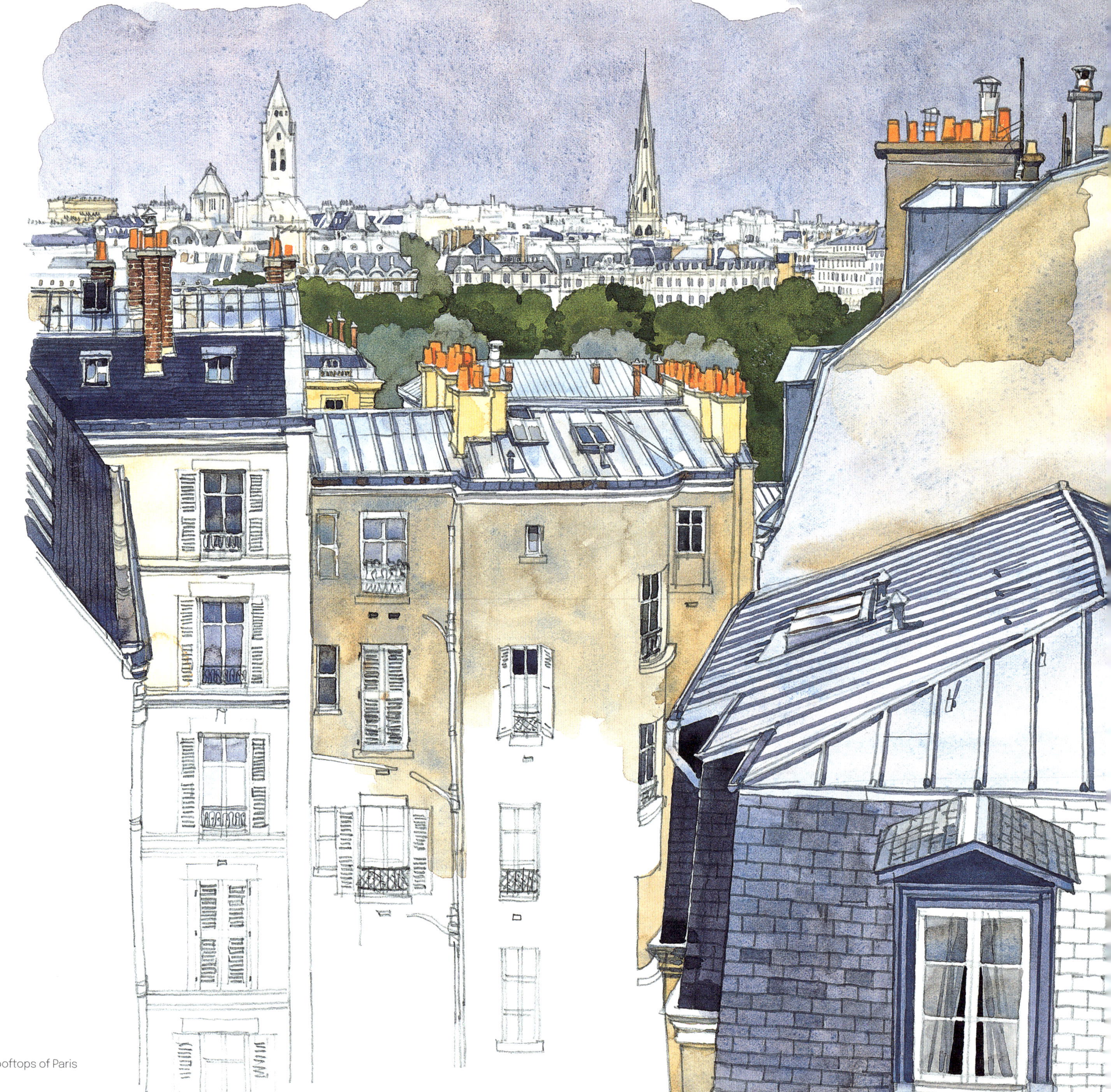

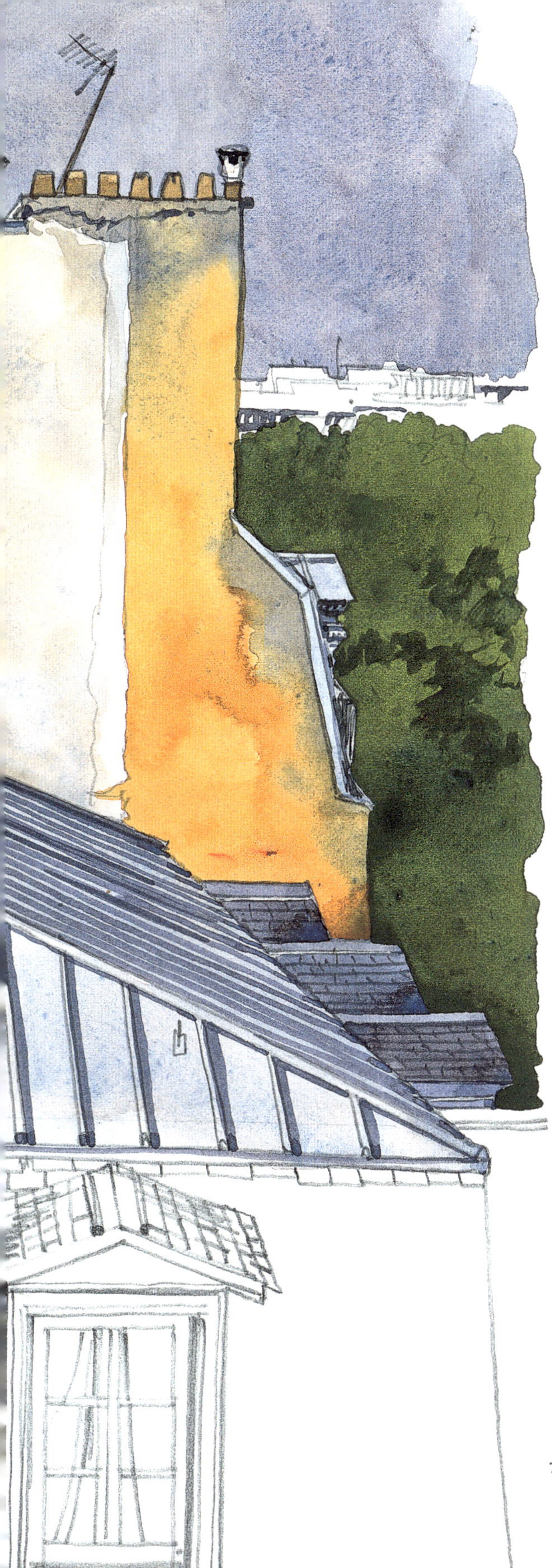

The hidden Seine

If our eyes were able,
to wander about at ease,
to roam among the chimney tops,
and among the far-off trees,
no alley would we see below,
but the river Seine in hiding,
invisible from where I'm perched.
From high in an attic dormer,
I imagine it beneath the green,
stretched out like a slumbering cat.

Postcard to a roof

From La Samaritaine, the distant views are like postcards. In one glance, we can see the Eiffel Tower, the Pont des Arts and a corner of the Louvre. But then, if we let our imagination be fired by the perspective, if our focal length is shortened, another world appears: an accumulation of honeycombed courtyards, a crenellated stack of chimneys, a delicate islet of tiles surmounted by a portico. A landscape trapped in the afternoon light, in which the spirit can wander.

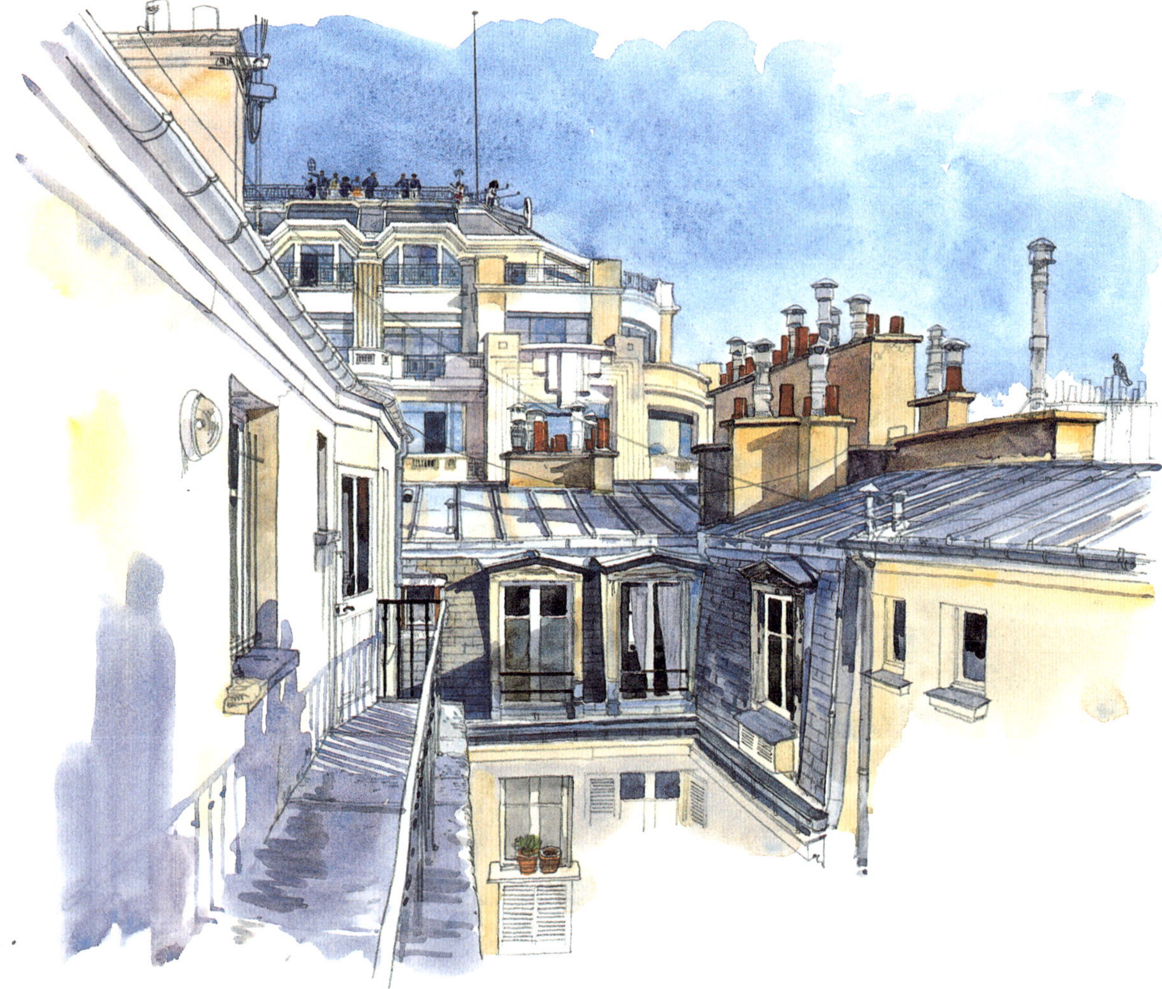

La Samaritaine seen from 1 Place de l'École. 1st arrondissement.

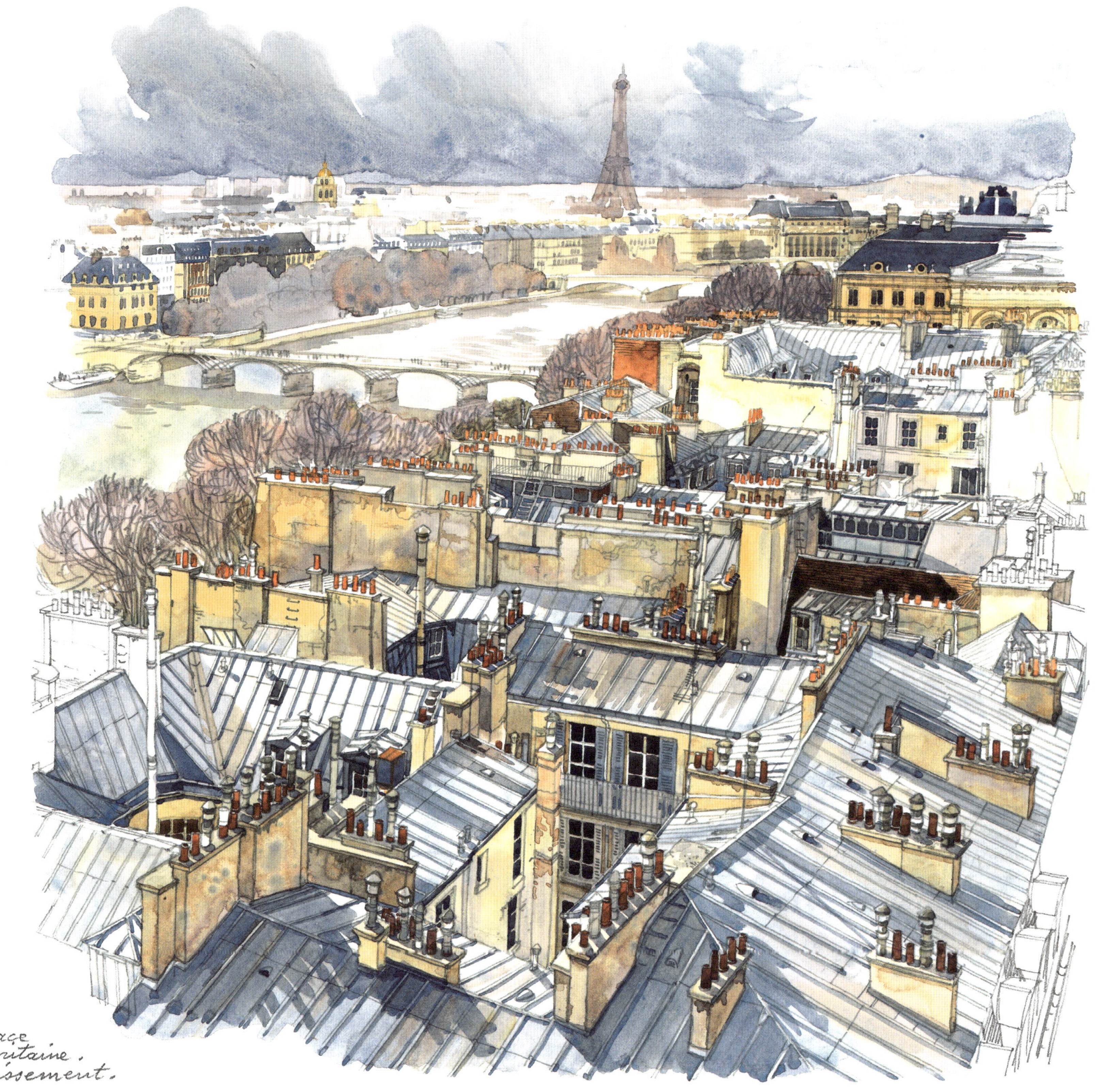
From up
on the terrace
of La Samaritaine.
1st arrondissement.

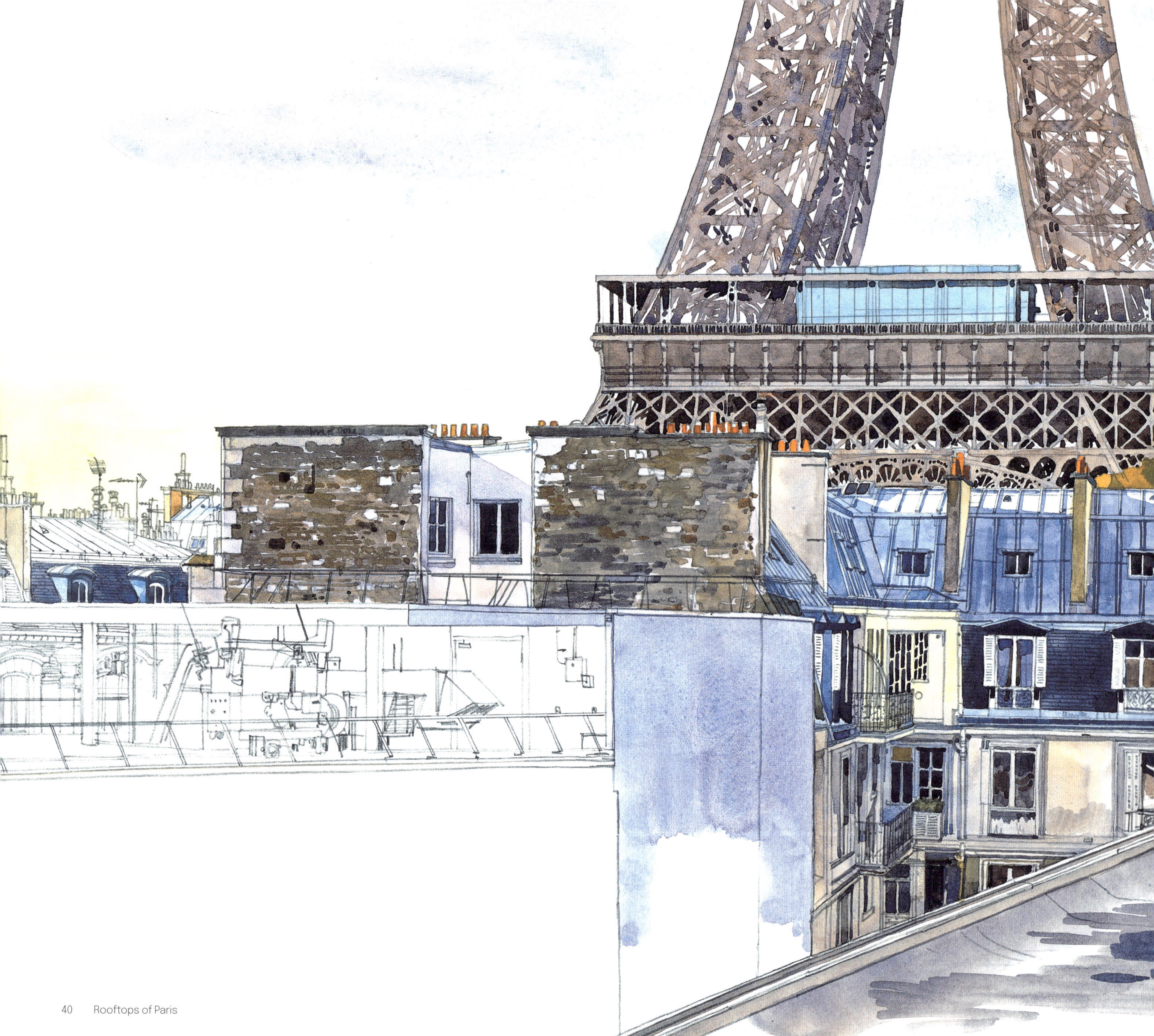

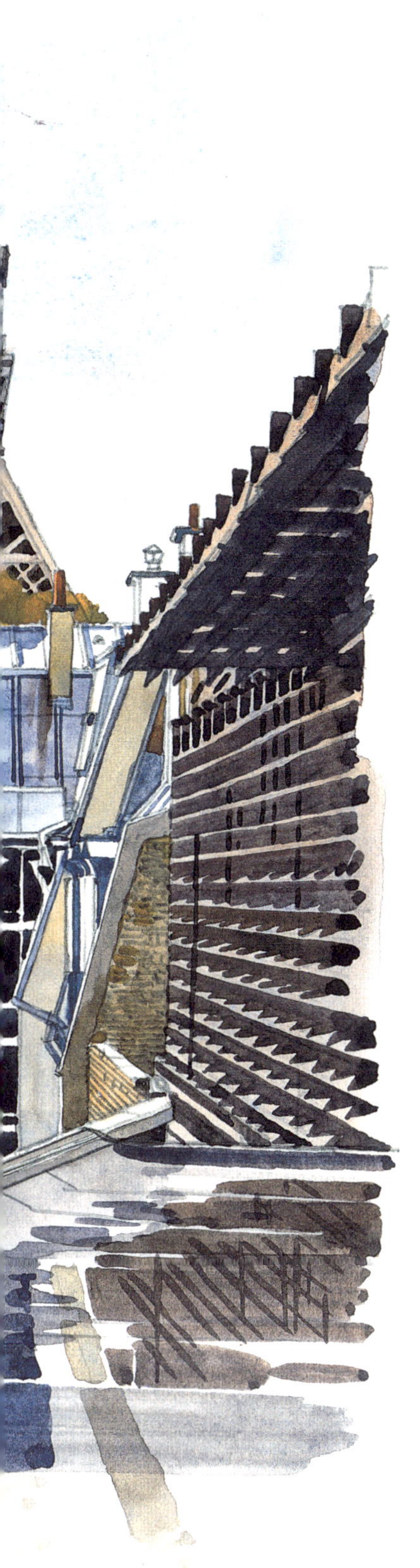

An indigenous art

Seen from the Musée du Quai Branly, here are the feet of one of the tallest totem poles in the world. Neither kachina nor tupilak, its interwoven metal is gigantic and menacing; its tip challenges the heavens. From up here, Monsieur Eiffel's creation never fails to disconcert the eye, familiar though we are with idols.

On the roof of the Musée
du Quai Branly. 7th arrondissement.

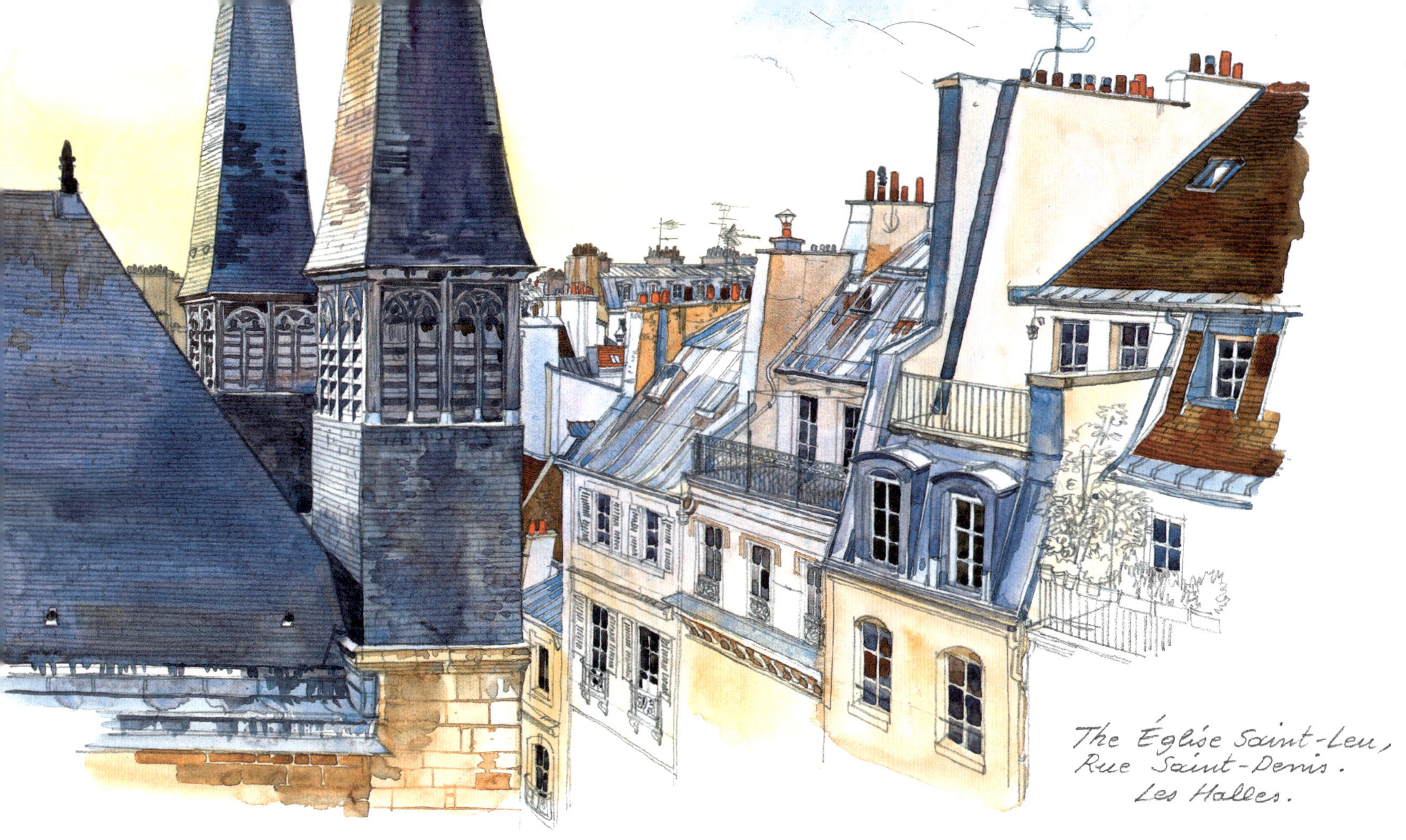

Guinguettes and cheap wine

At the tollgates, where those who were refused entry to the city once made their homes, a veritable kingdom flourished: illegal traders, small-time innkeepers, smugglers of cheap wine to be drunk on the spot or taken away, assorted low-lifes and prostitutes, ruffians with dodgy names, pushy policemen, shady merchants, all pressing up against the walls of Paris. Sometimes, the air above the Porte Saint-Denis or elsewhere was filled with lost souls, traces of wine fumes, words, wrongs that will never be put right, and laughter from the rooftops too loud ever to disappear.

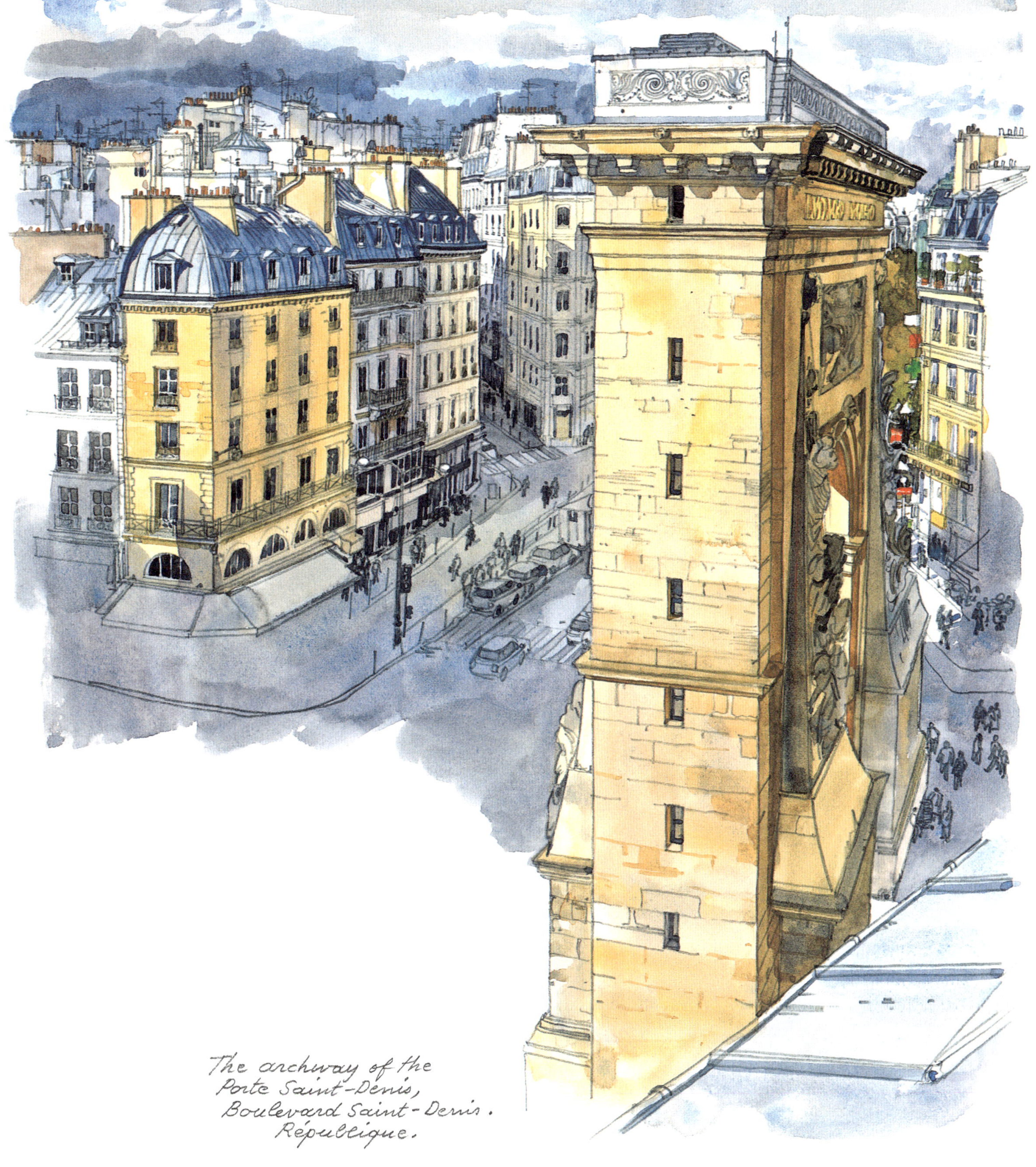

The archway of the
Porte Saint-Denis,
Boulevard Saint-Denis.
République.

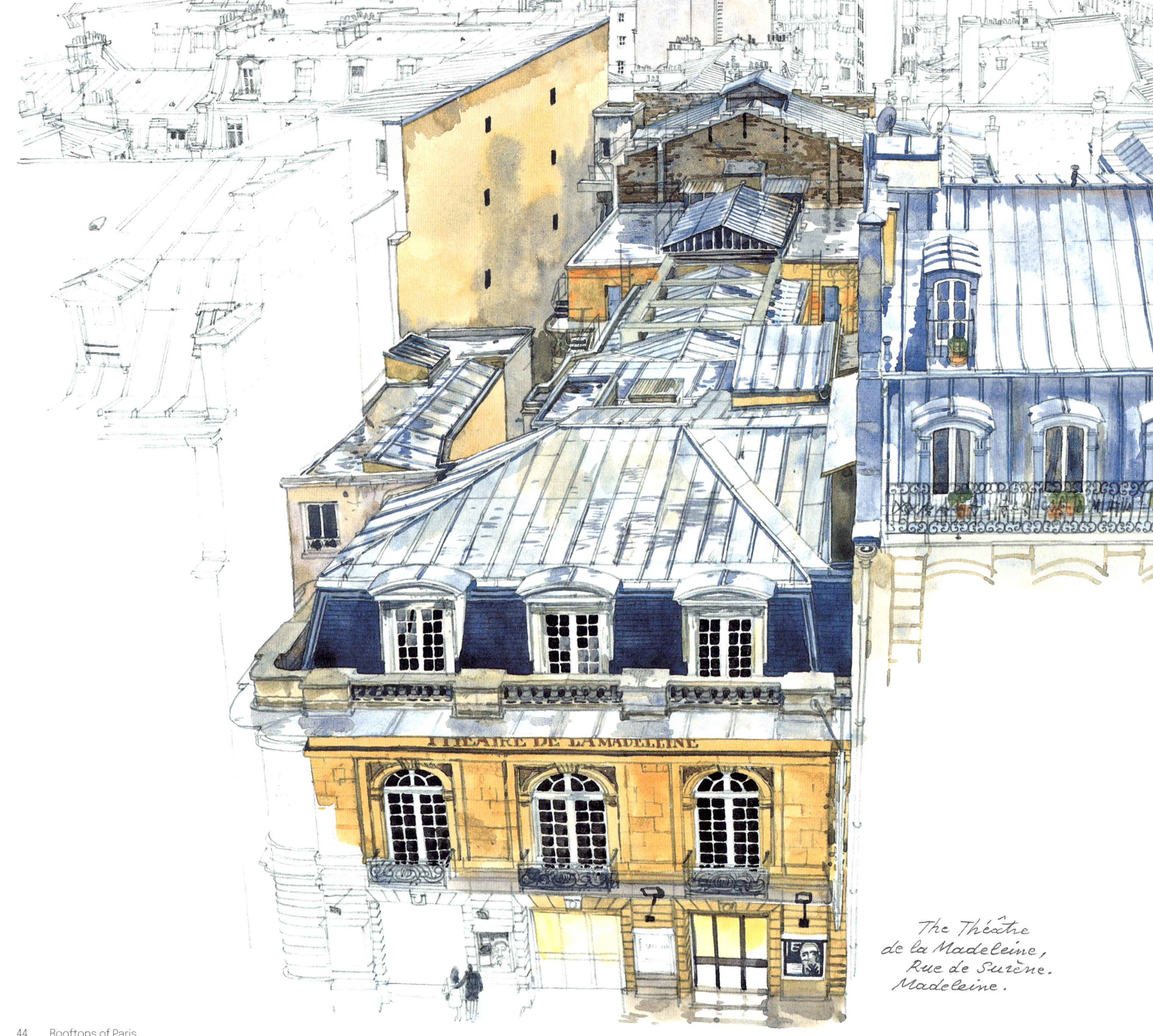

The Théâtre
de la Madeleine,
Rue de Surène.
Madeleine.

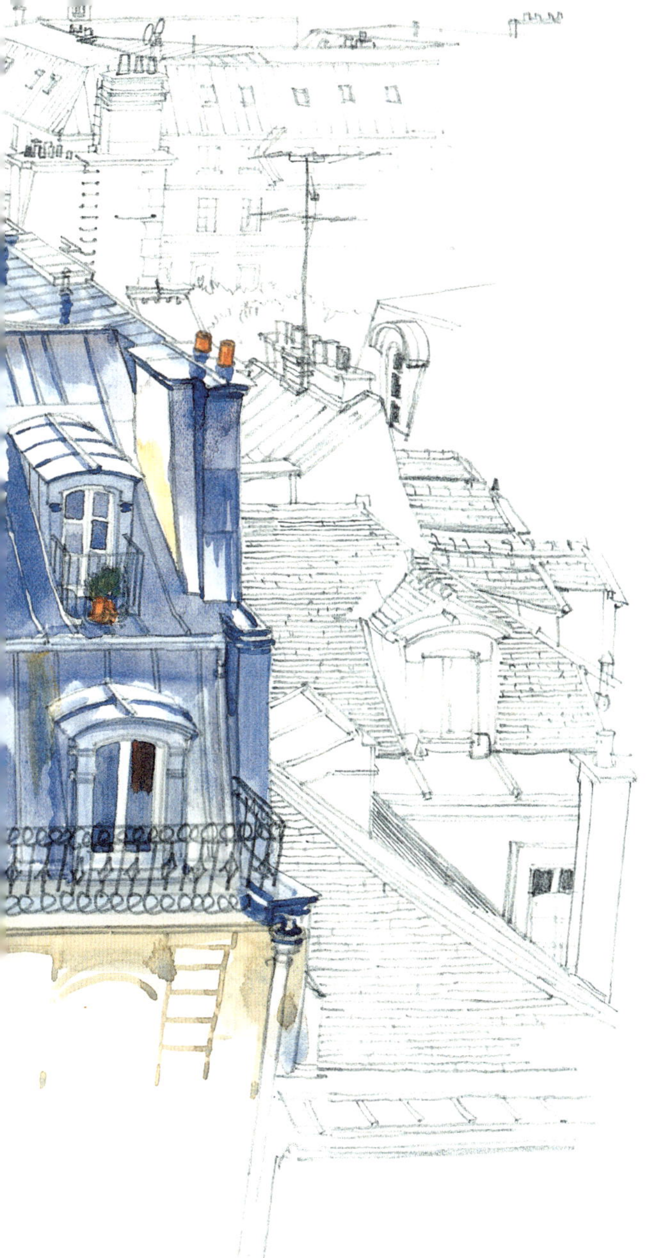

Guitry's La Madeleine

Some ghosts dress better than others. Never at rest in their white sheets, they laugh eerily and slam doors. At the Théâtre de la Madeleine, few remember Pagnol; it was here that Sacha Guitry became a legend. Making regular appearances, this ghostly figure with hat and pince-nez can sometimes be seen haunting the stage or taking a stroll along the gutters, repeating over and over again that actors must be taken seriously, and adding, as he disappears, leaving behind a whiff of cigar smoke: "To be Parisian is not to be born in Paris, but to be reborn there."

Room
with a view

In late 1831, drifting down like an autumn leaf, Frédéric Chopin arrived in Paris, still disorientated by the uprisings in his homeland, with a little soil in his pockets taken from the Poland he would never see again. He first made his home at 27 Boulevard Poissonnière, just beneath the roof. "Many people envy my view, but none my stairs," he wrote in a letter. From the balcony, the ultimate luxury, he could see Montmartre and the Panthéon. Up there, he was able to draw breath, looking over the Paris that he was set to conquer, with an urgent desire to live and breathe in harmony with the city while there was still time.

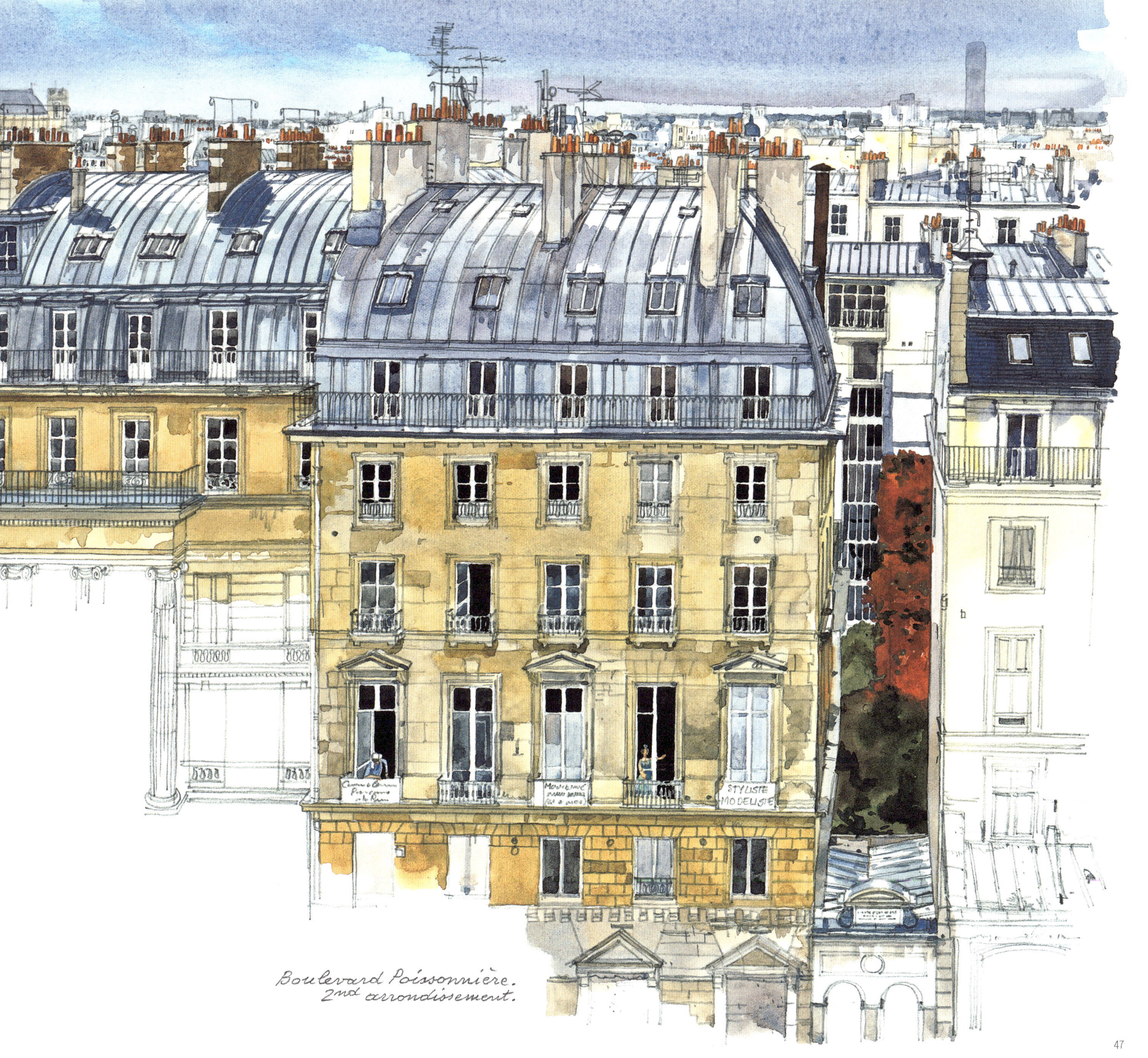

Boulevard Poissonnière.
2ème arrondissement.

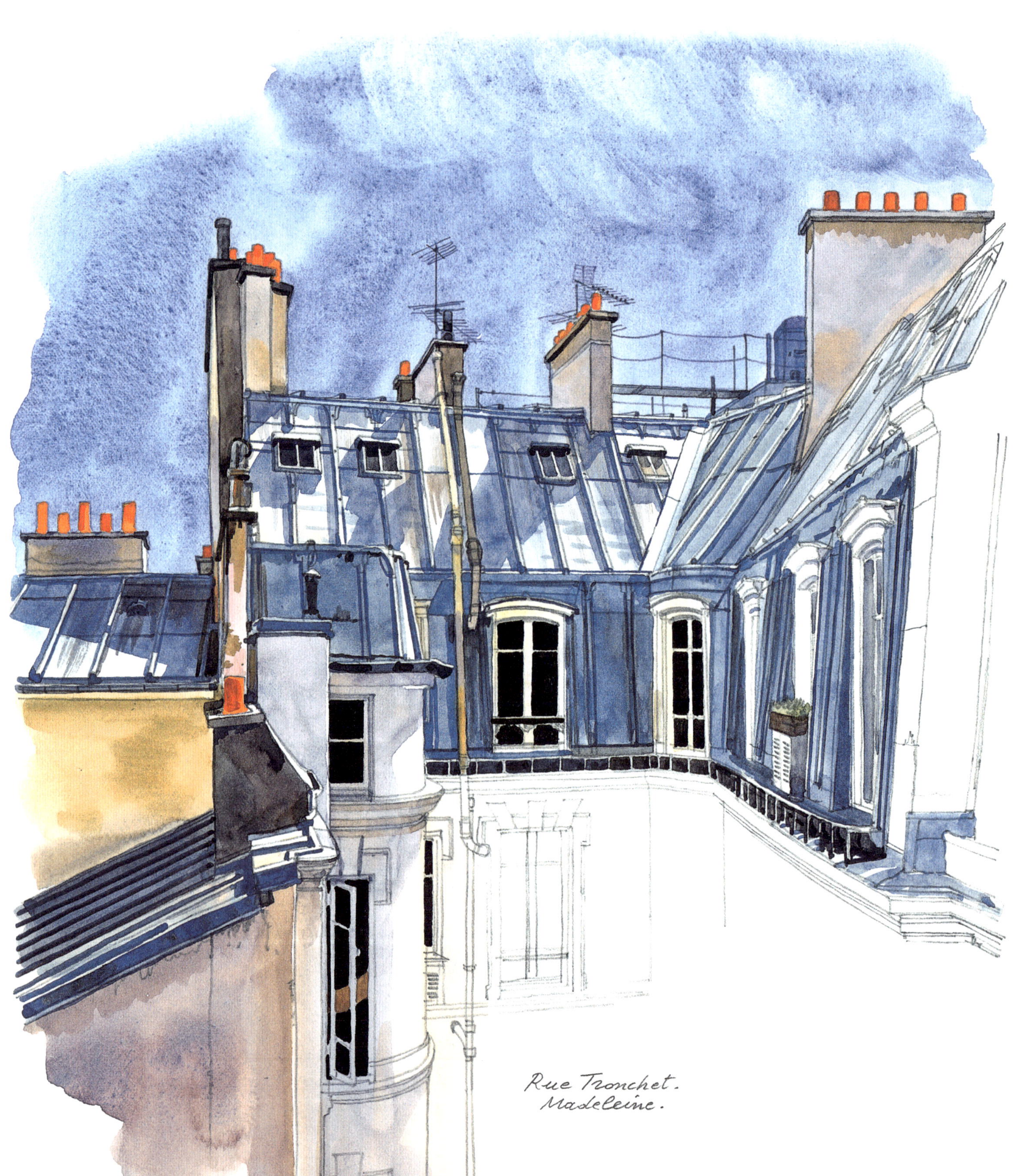

Rue Tronchet.
Madeleine.

Paris for a blonde

Under the sun, the roofs turn into mirrors or zinc tabletops. Our eyes wander slowly across the scene. High up, the chimneys are shaped like bishops' mitres. We notice other concrete headwear, and the cowls like little gnomes. We imagine ourselves having a picnic on the ridge of the sloping roofs, surrounded by a few plants. A few birds – the less grey ones – will come to peck at the crumbs. The melody of a song from the past wafts upwards and suddenly a blonde girl gets up and dances in the sun. The old refrains continue as evening falls. And gradually, we feel a little more love in the air.

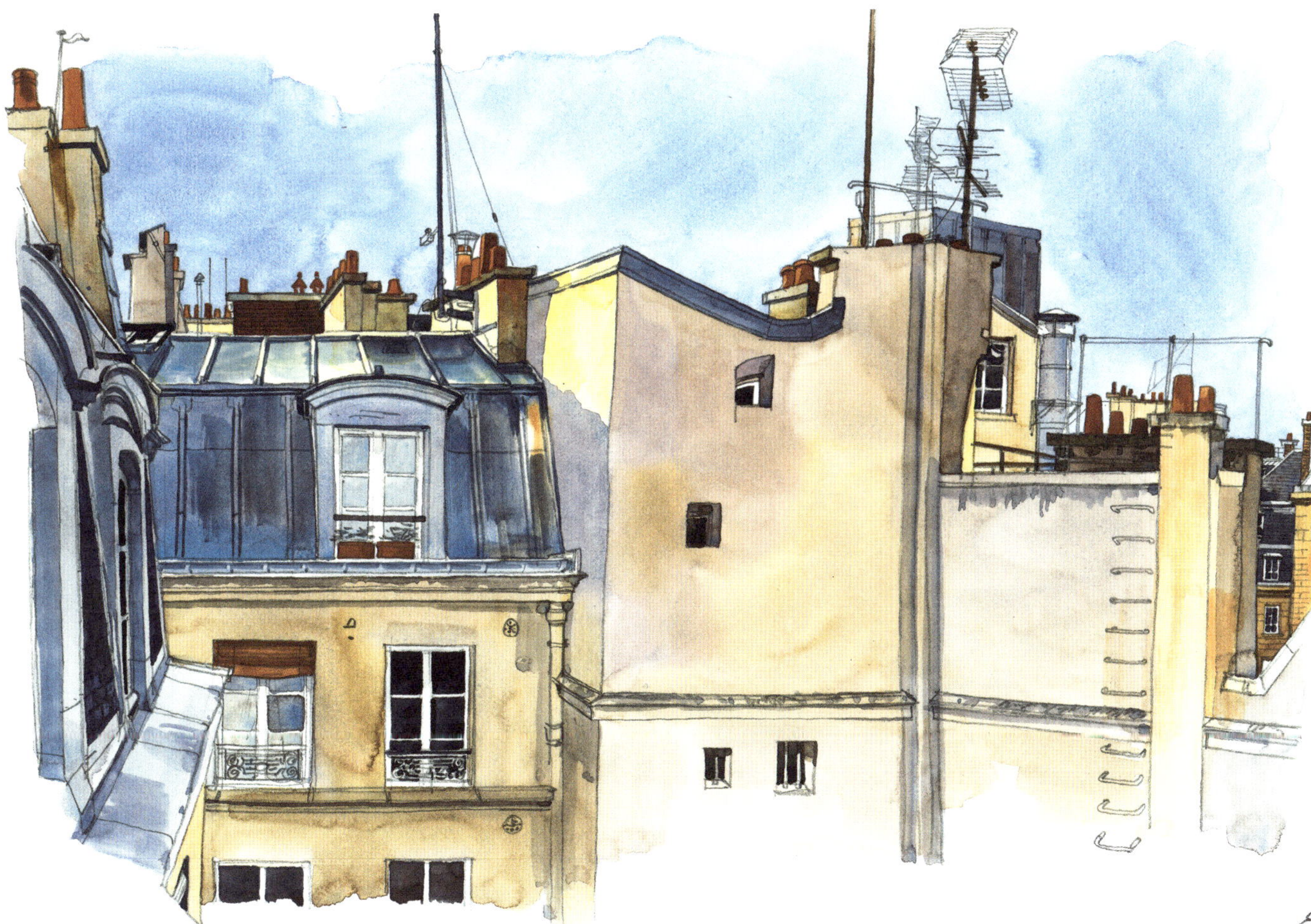

Commuters

At ground level, they are commuters.
Seen from up on the roof, they form
dense ant-like swarms, as shoulders
jostle, caps and hats meet, heads of hair
move as if in a wind that isn't really there.
I contemplate these chasers after time.
I steal an hour from them, they take only
a moment from me. People stream out
of the metro at Bourse and Opéra, in no
particular formation, frozen in the early
morning; but from this height, what a
beguiling sight, like the surface of fabric
in the sunlight! The commuters follow
their lives like people throwing a dice
time after time, without ever playing the
game. Minor introspections are their fate
from the moment dawn breaks. At times,
some of them pause briefly and seem,
from up here, to have a moment of doubt,
before rearranging their briefcases
and setting off again, caught in the act
of existing in the world's very flesh.

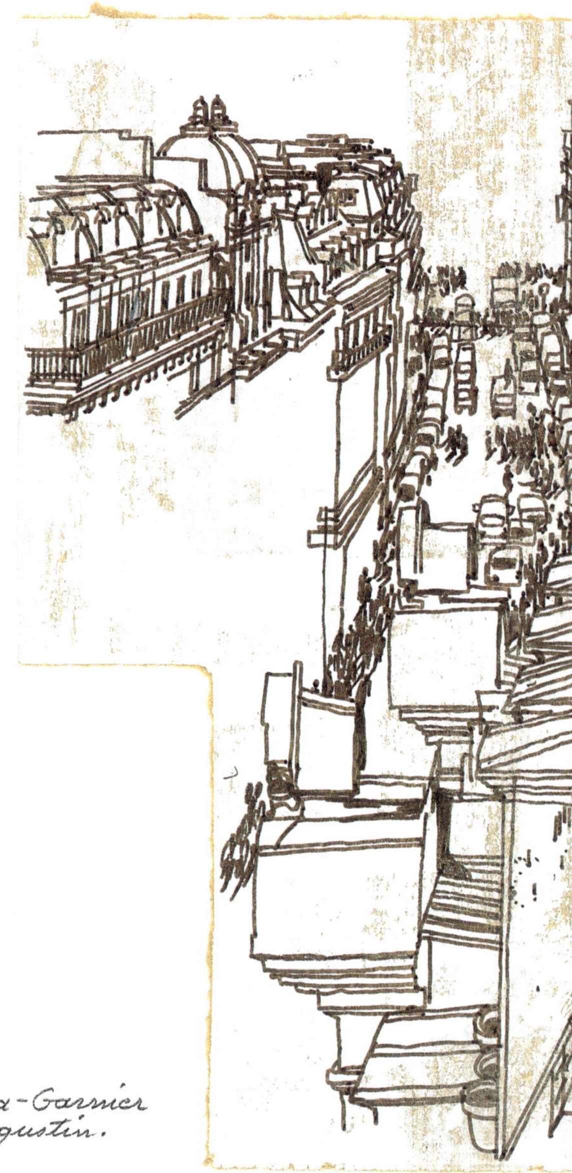

La Défense, the Opéra-Garnier
seen from Rue Saint-Augustin.
Opéra.

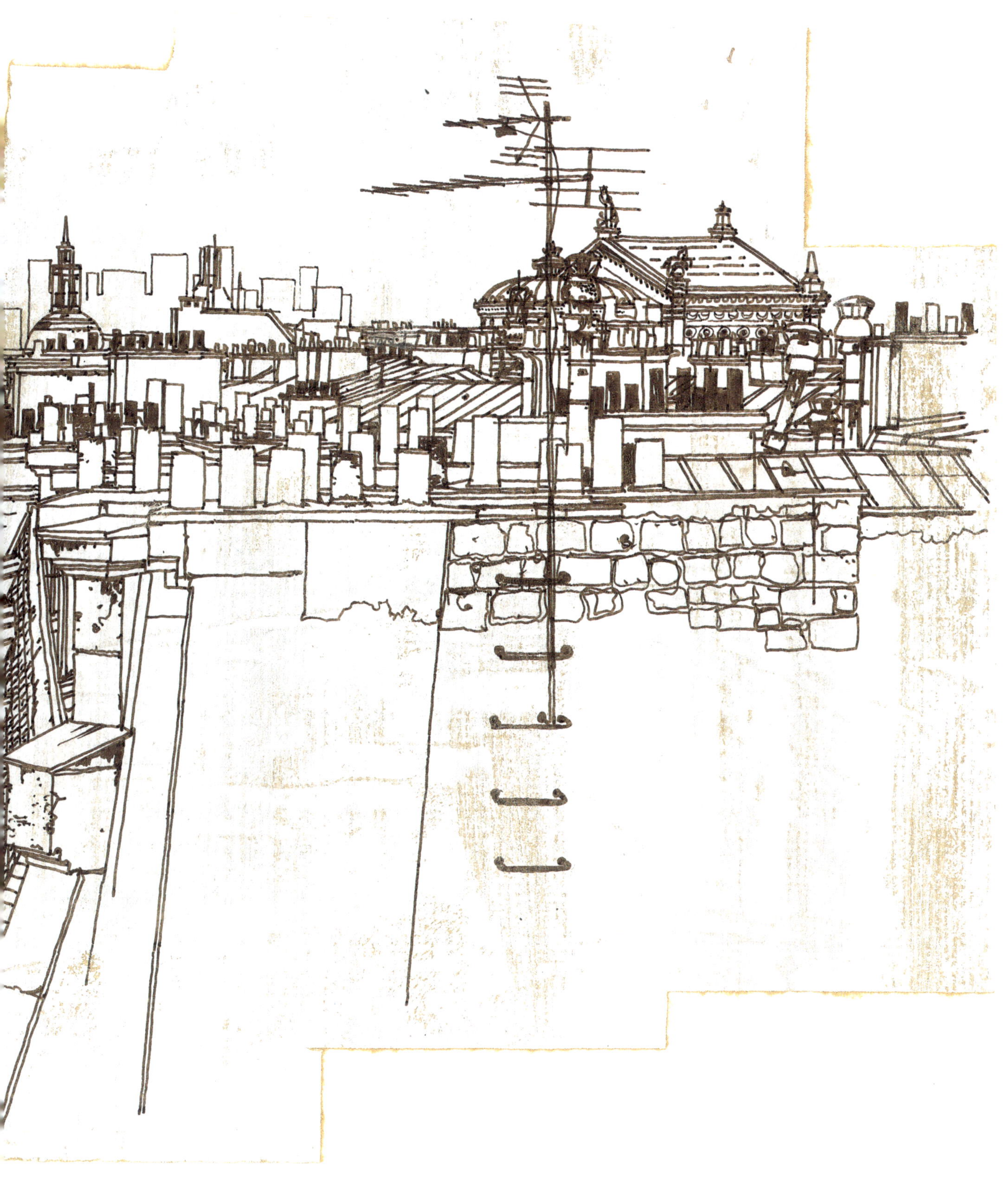

To the music-loving bee

The honey of Paris is priceless, people say. But here the bees are music lovers. They swarm to the latest concerto, abuzz with debate over the merits of Mozart's or Dvořák's flights of fancy. Long after their ancestors displayed their finery in the Jardin du Luxembourg more than a hundred years ago, these sunny insects have made their home on the roof of the Opéra Garnier. Their penthouse hives have their own musical scores, and the nectar that these beauties seek out, far from the pesticides used in the countryside, is said to produce a honey purer than that from anywhere else. When a double bass is bored with playing or a minuet goes round in circles, the bees compose a fugue, flying off to the lime trees in the Palais Royal, seeking out pagoda trees, even lavender. Honey, like music, is enriched by contrasts, mixtures and detours. Beneath the roof and all around, both singers and insects improvise. Not the flight of the bee, but the song of a journey from the soul to the ear, from flower to mouth.

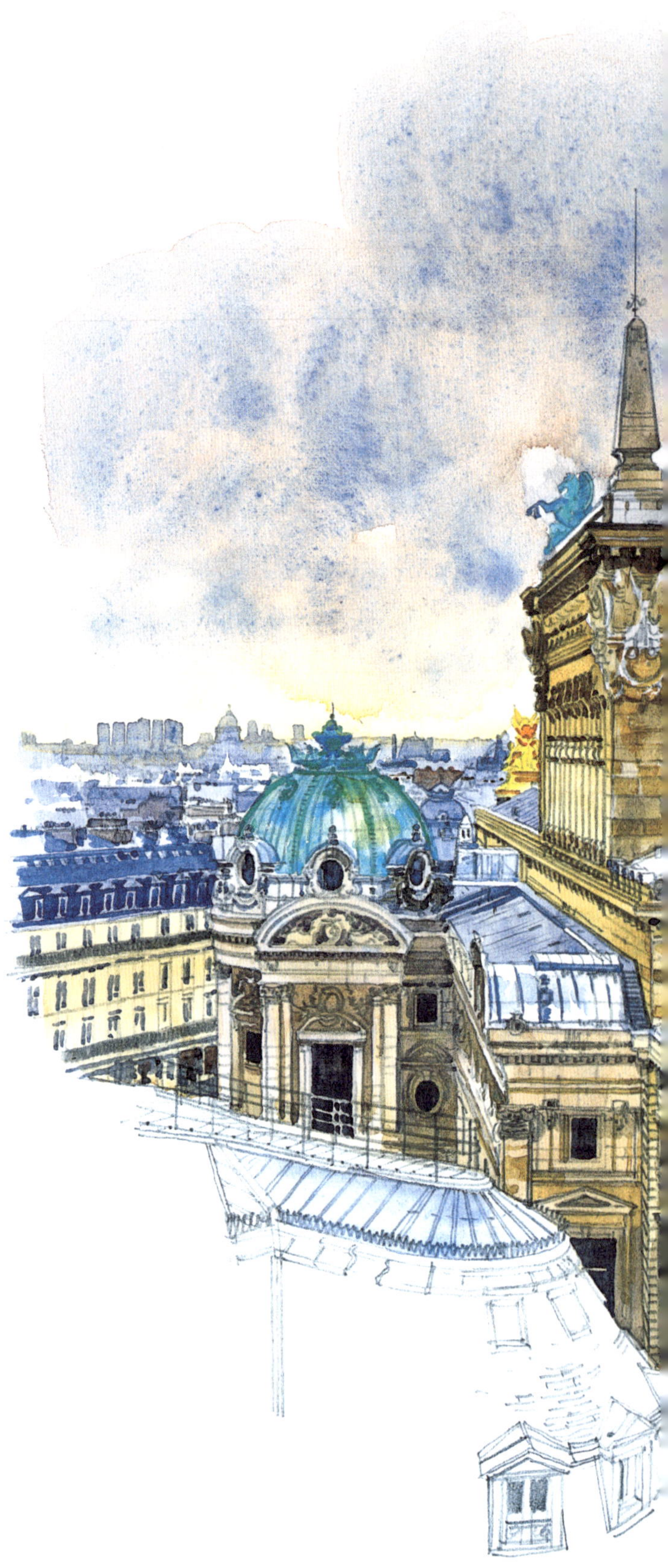

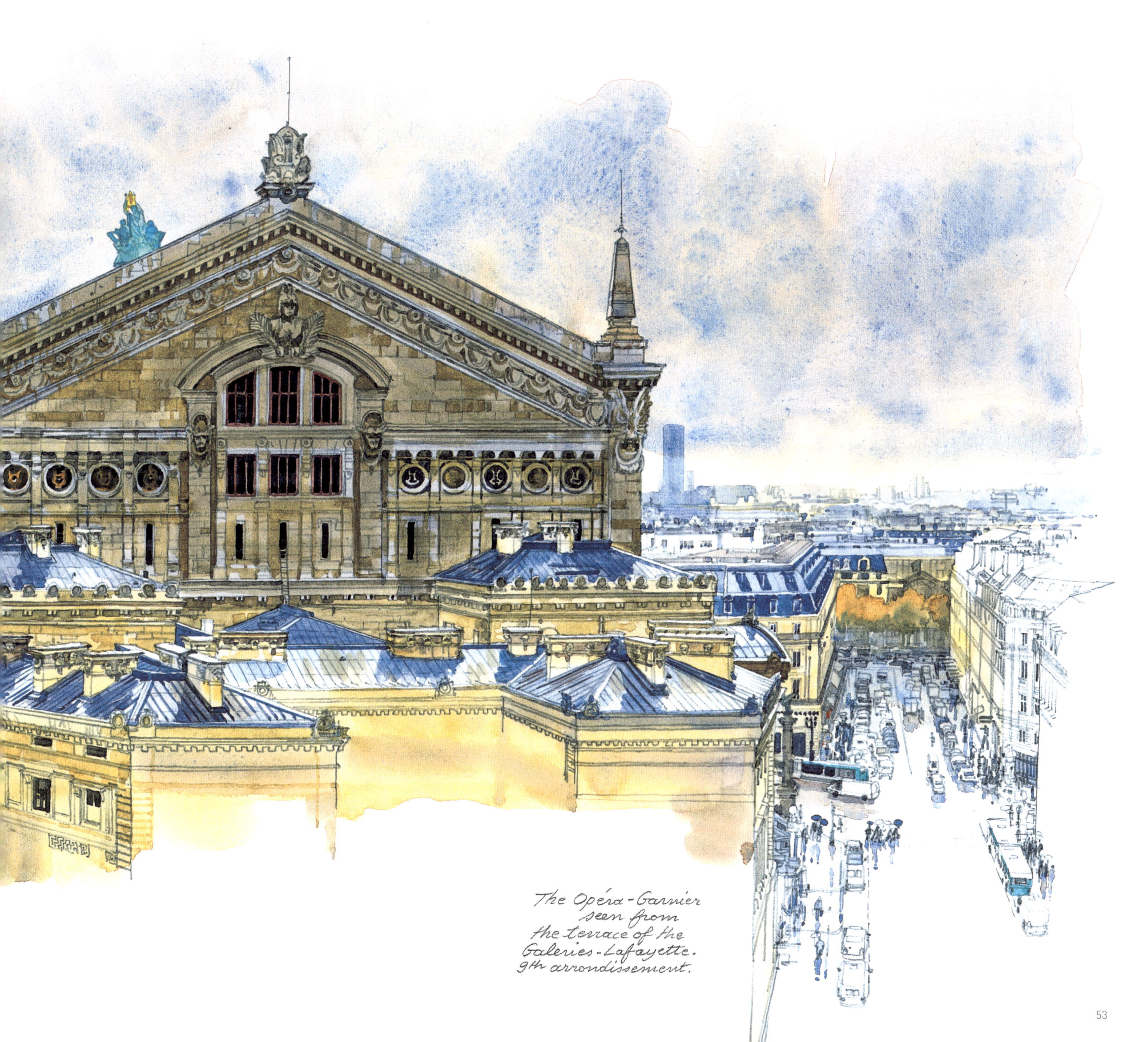

The Opéra-Garnier
seen from
the terrace of the
Galeries-Lafayette.
9th arrondissement.

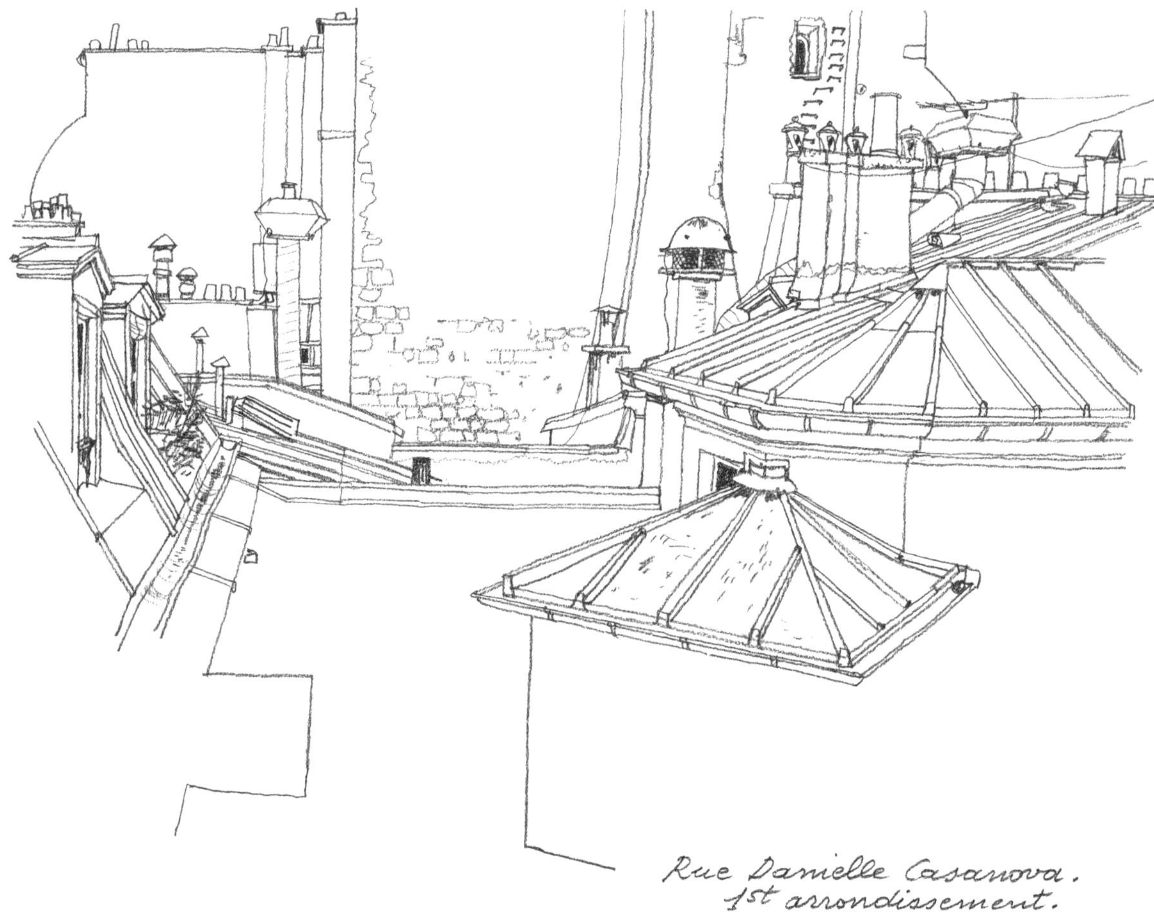

Stacks of chimneys

These chimney pots, lined up
like onions or a battle formation,
are not an army on the run,
nor forgotten pawns from a chess game,
nor neglected skittles as yet unfallen,
nor glasses toasting themselves
at a party of invisible guests,
nor tubes for unlikely messages
in an old pneumatic mail system,
nor sockets for missing lamps intended
for mystics to light up the sky.
These chimney pots are simply notes
from a seven- or eight-line score,
a minuet or, even better, a fugue.

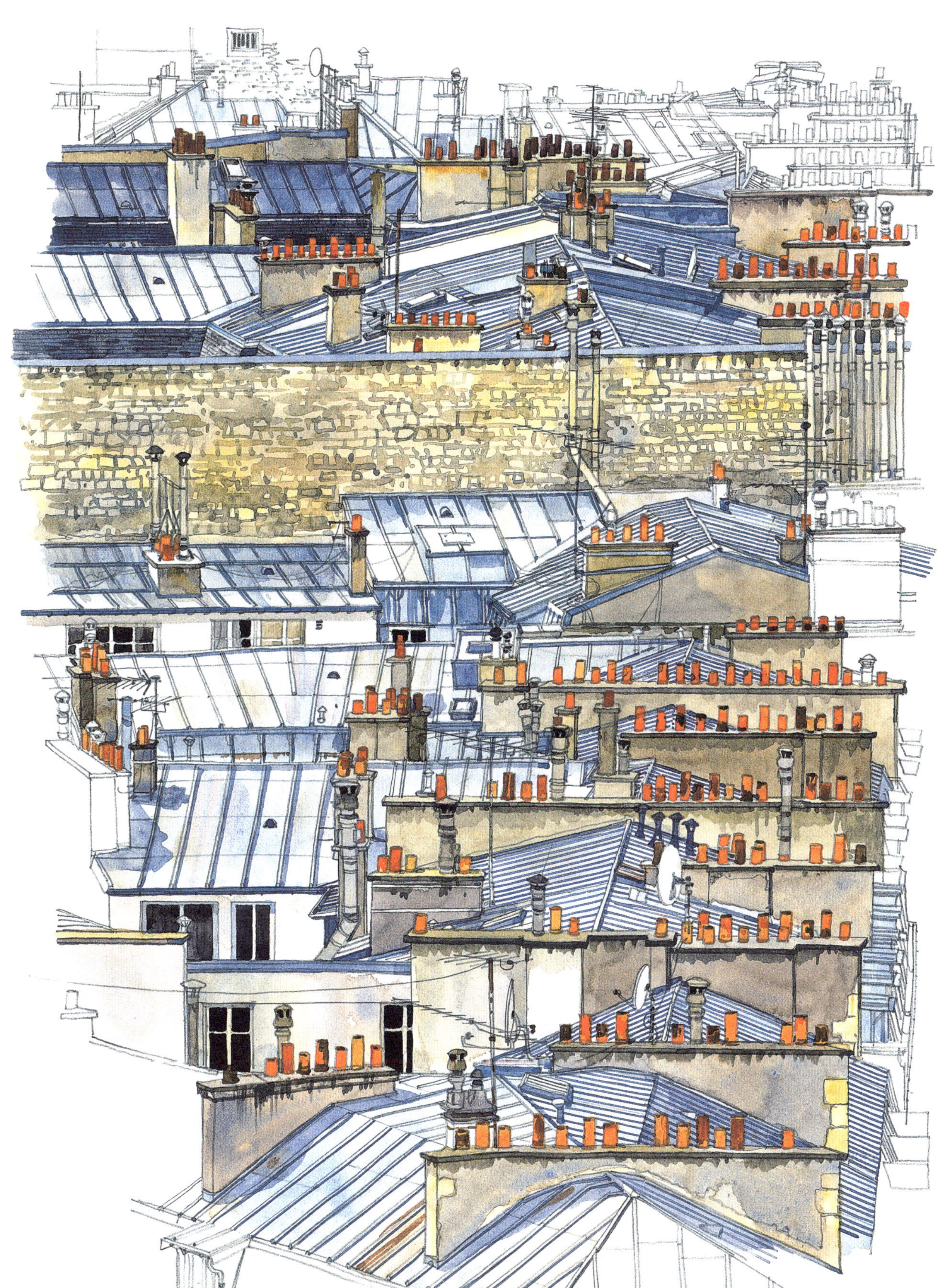

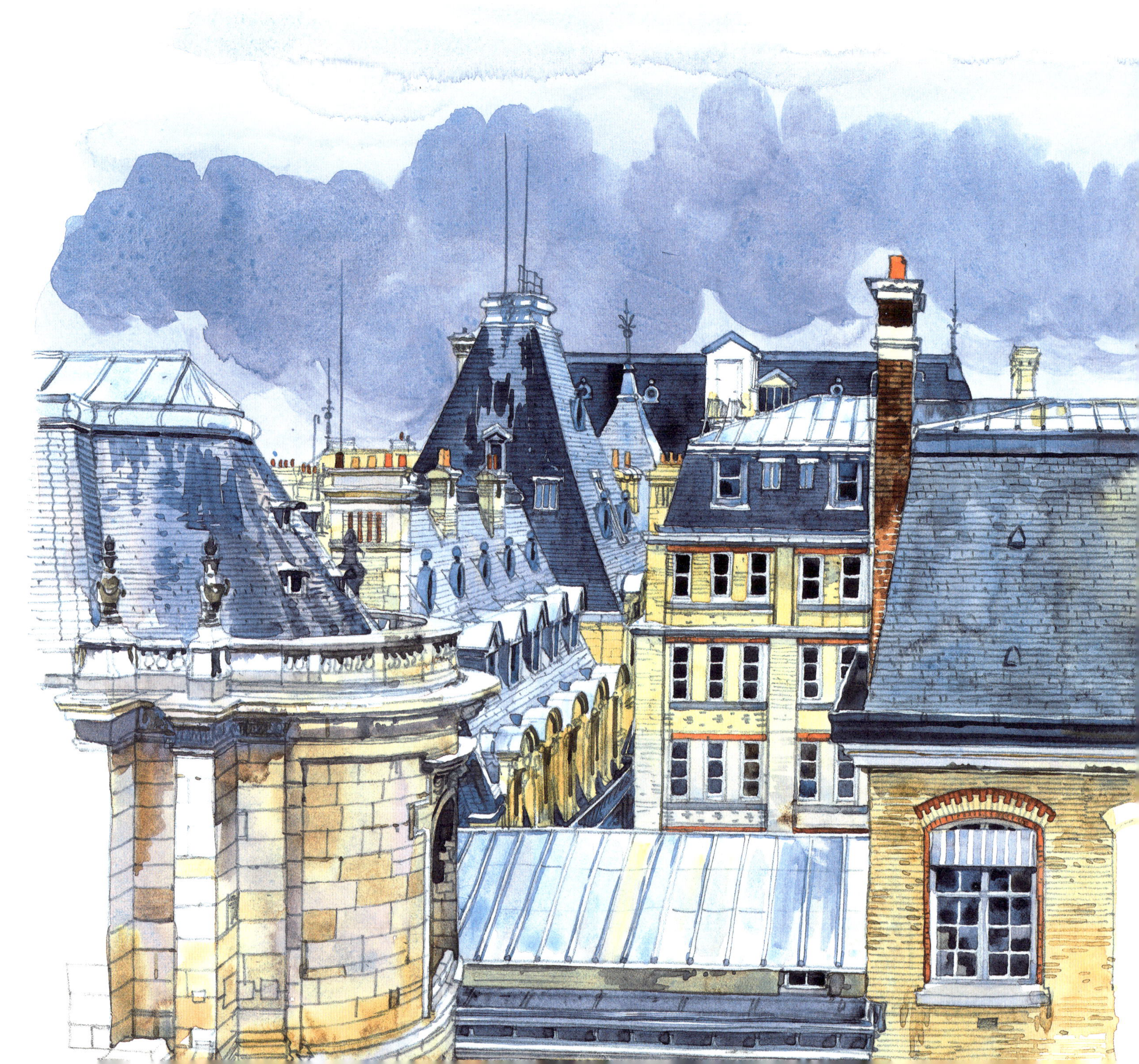

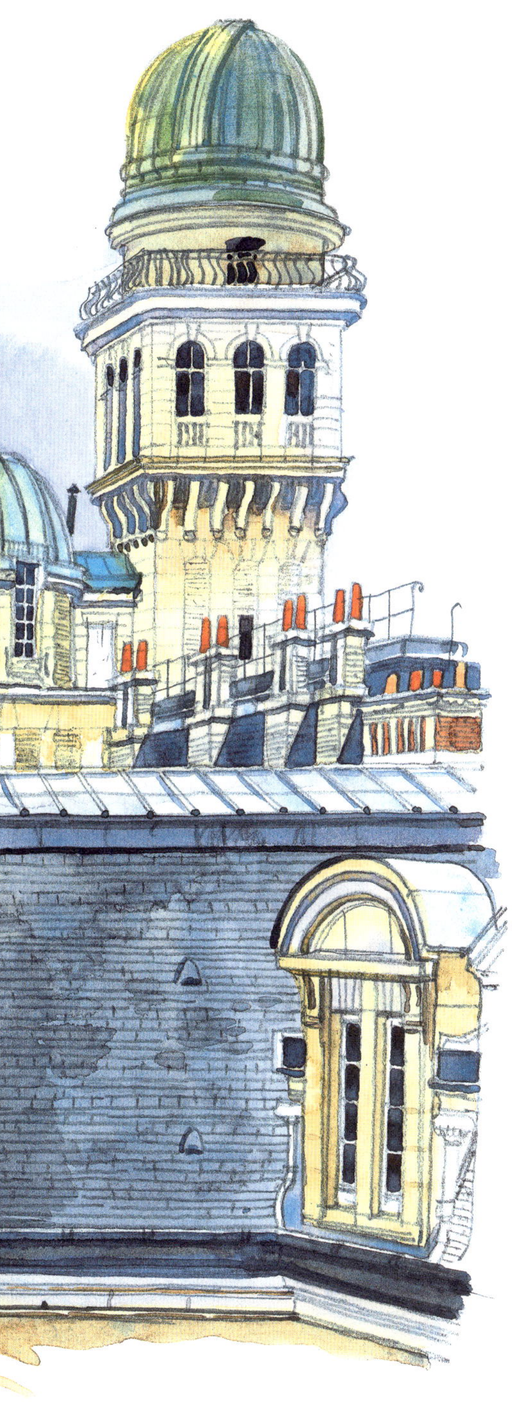

The favour of the stars

Paris is the City of Light. Everybody knows that. And the city of five-star hotels. But what of the heavens above? For this, you need to go for a look around the roof of the Observatoire. Under the dome, the openings are for a telescope that has served well over time. The instrument was not that of a Cyclops, a creature with one eye. It was here that one Monsieur Cassini, as much magician as optician and astronomer, created the first map of the moon. With his lens, one perfectly clear night, he observed the satellites of Saturn and the way its rings were arranged. From up on this roof, a voice seems forever to ring out with the words: "This is the Grand Equatorial speaking, please dear stars, can we meet, throw caution to the wind, and shine over Paris for a moment, City of Light within a sea of lights."

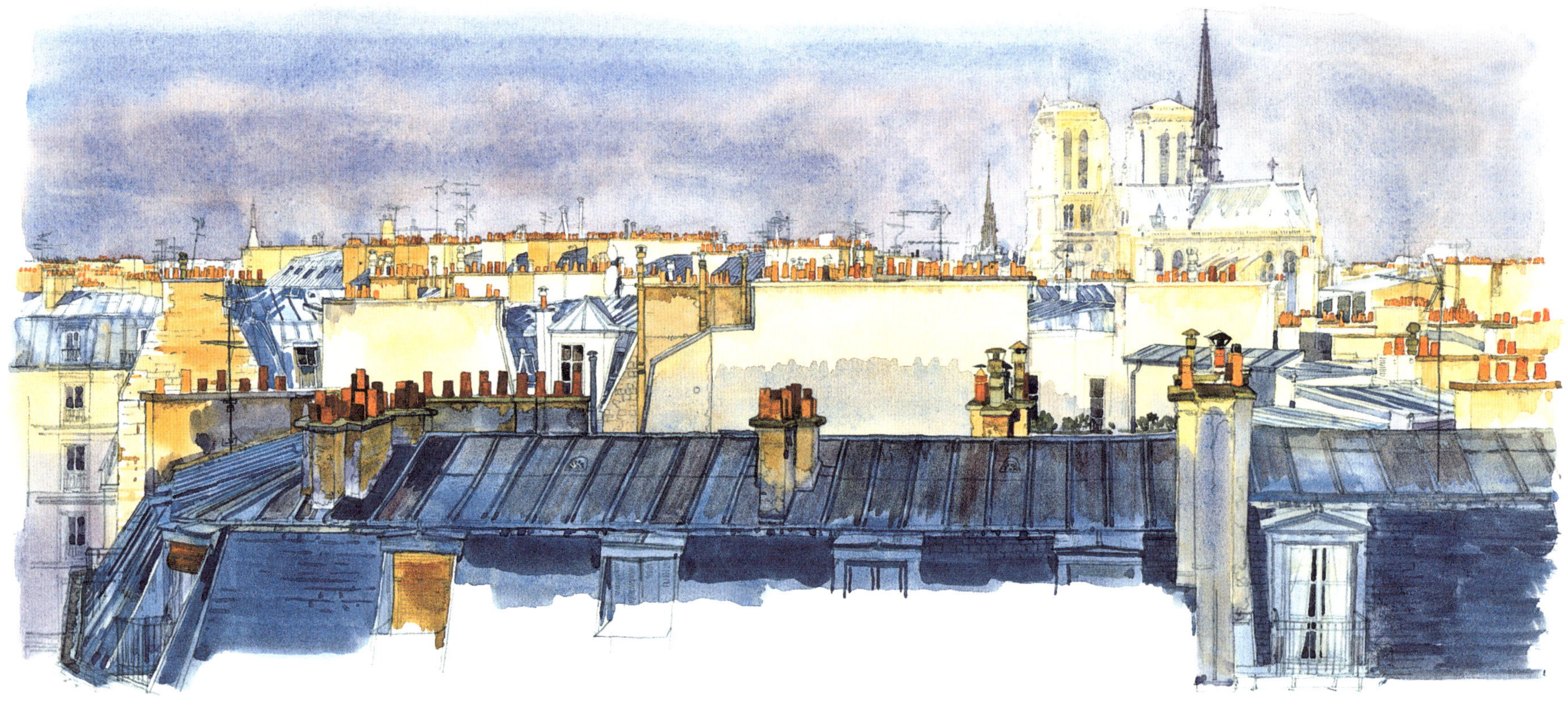

Portrait of a sightless person

The blind man who speaks of the roofs never mentions the silence of his eyes. His voice is high enough to rise above the pavement. His expressive hands, especially, evoke curves and gables. His fingers mimic crumbling, rubble, sometimes in contrast to solid stone or metal arches. His profession? When asked, he replies sky tuner or tightrope walker. His palm looks scarred in one place. Touching the roofs, sometimes clawing like a cat, caused the damage to his hands. Or at least that's what he says. He tells anyone who cares to listen that he played at being immortal on the dome of the Panthéon. He even likes to recount how he spent a night chatting with the gargoyles high above Notre-Dame's nave. "Only the birds never lie," he adds, gently smoothing his mop of hair.

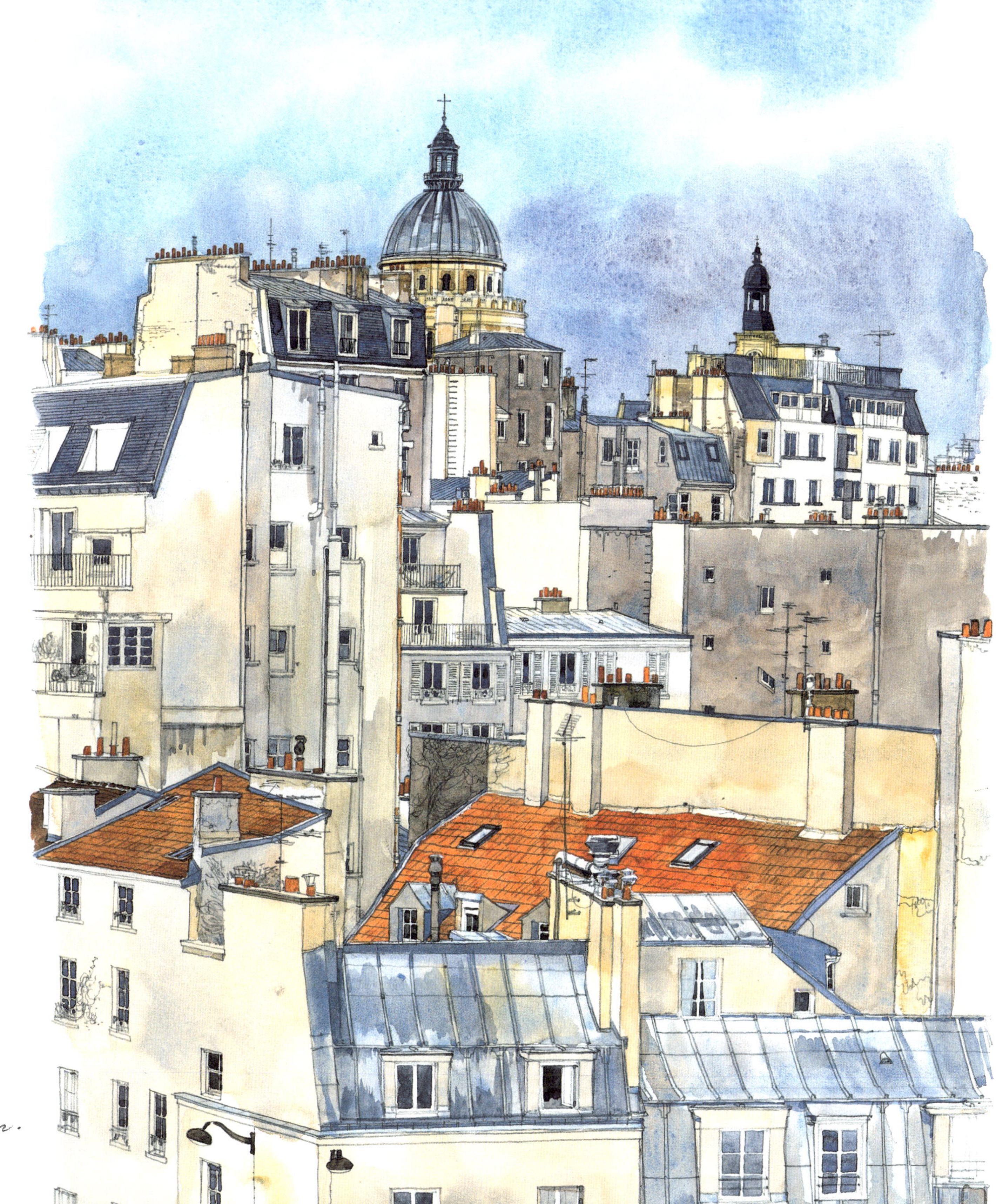

The Panthéon seen from the Faculty of Sciences of Jussieu. Quartier Latin.

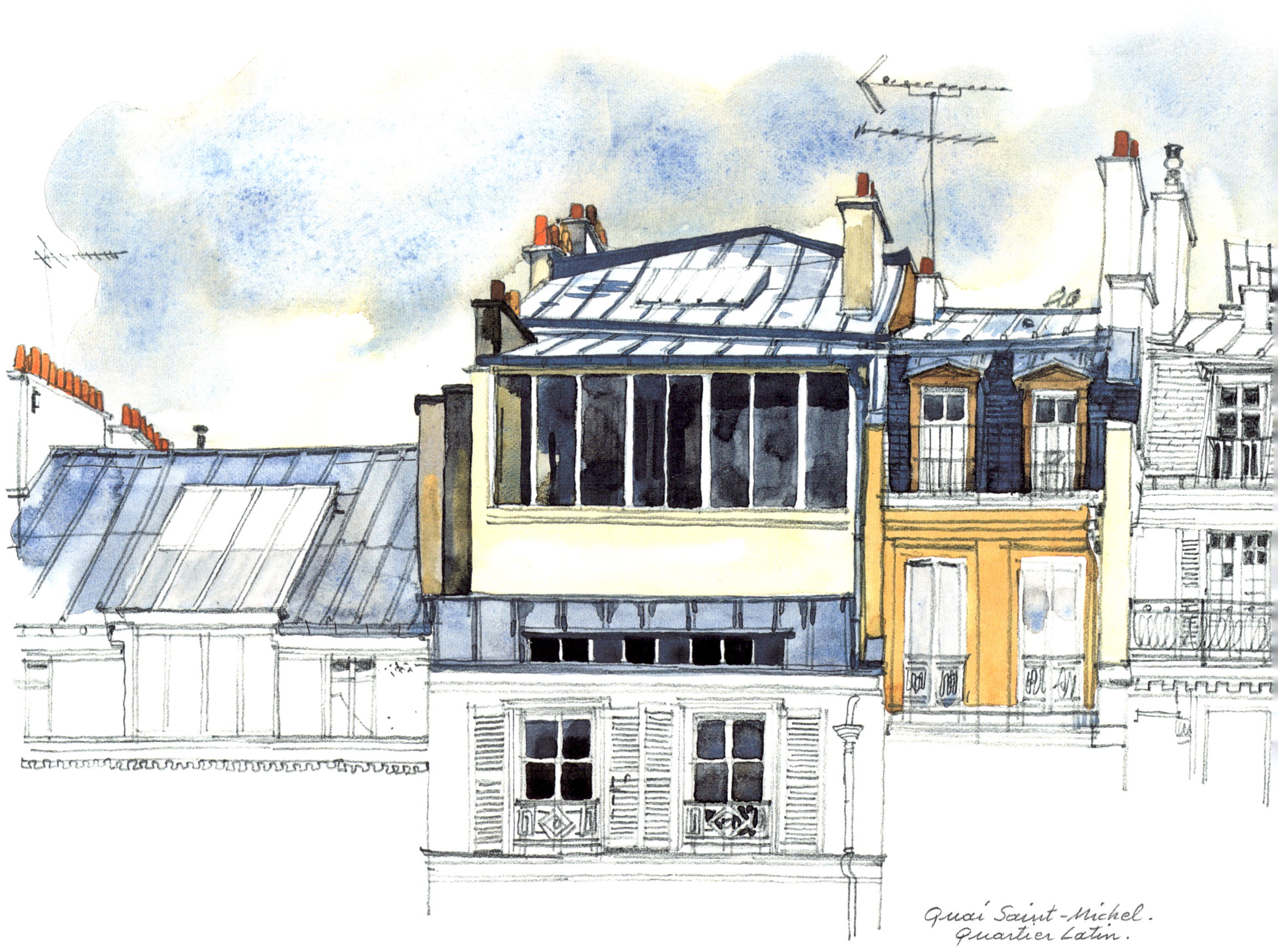

Quai Saint-Michel.
Quartier Latin.

Chez Matisse

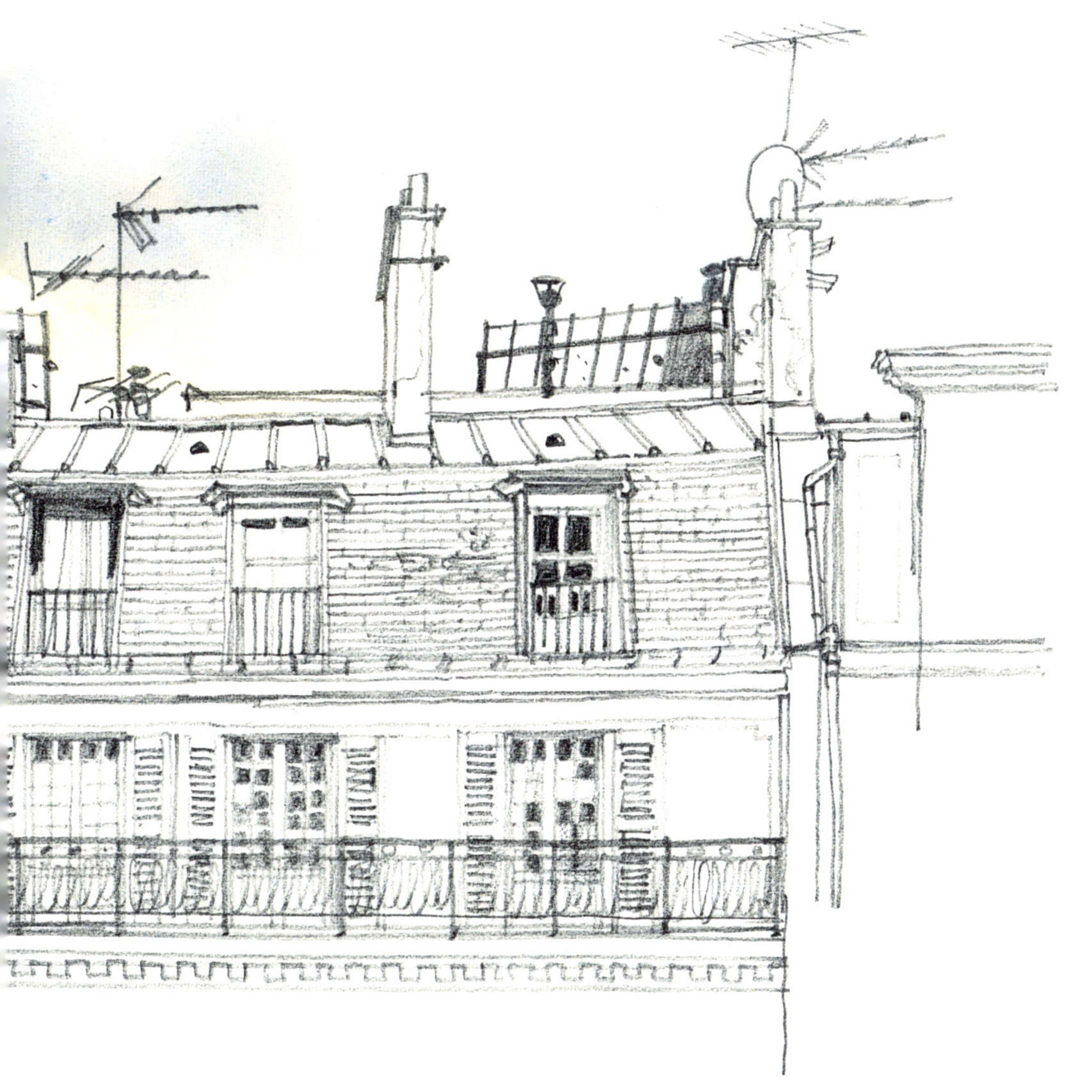

Matisse is asleep, leaning against the window. He's twenty-six, and elsewhere life is short – it's already wartime. The warmth of the morning touches the studio's large panes of glass. Matisse awakens, lifts his hand, listening, as if to music, to the tune his fingers trace in the air, playing with matter. Matisse opens his eyes, thinking of fields less bloody, purely chromatic.

"The colour of light!" he will say, leaning like a tree towards the Pont Saint-Michel. At that time, he used to liken himself to a pear tree and Picasso to an apple tree. Matisse takes up his brushes, paints a nude, counts doves. Happiness moves from breast to beak, or feasts on a simple goldfish bowl. Still life, odd-looking clusters of shells, the Seine below, a sudden blue, and a bridge now endowed with feet the colour of fawn. Matisse looks at his hand, full of life. He applies ink to paper, then, ignoring the window frame, with large brushstrokes he invites Notre-Dame to step up to his corner of the sky where, on the roof at number 19, his chest against the window, he finally admits to feeling dizzy.

Shakespeare & Company, Paris

On a grey, drizzly morning, wedged between two taller buildings, the little house, weathered by time, breathes through its roof. From afar, it looks like a stage set, a cardboard decoration, put up and forgotten, the actors all gone, struck down perhaps as if in a Shakespearean tragedy. The house seems to consist of a staircase, with protruding windows, leading up towards a slightly shakey roof; it's masquerading as a tumbledown shack to hide the treasures within. The important thing, it seems, is to have pushed up towards a ray of light, to have sprouted like a plant and flowered through the roof, where the eye can linger and the afternoon sun can bring a friendly warmth.

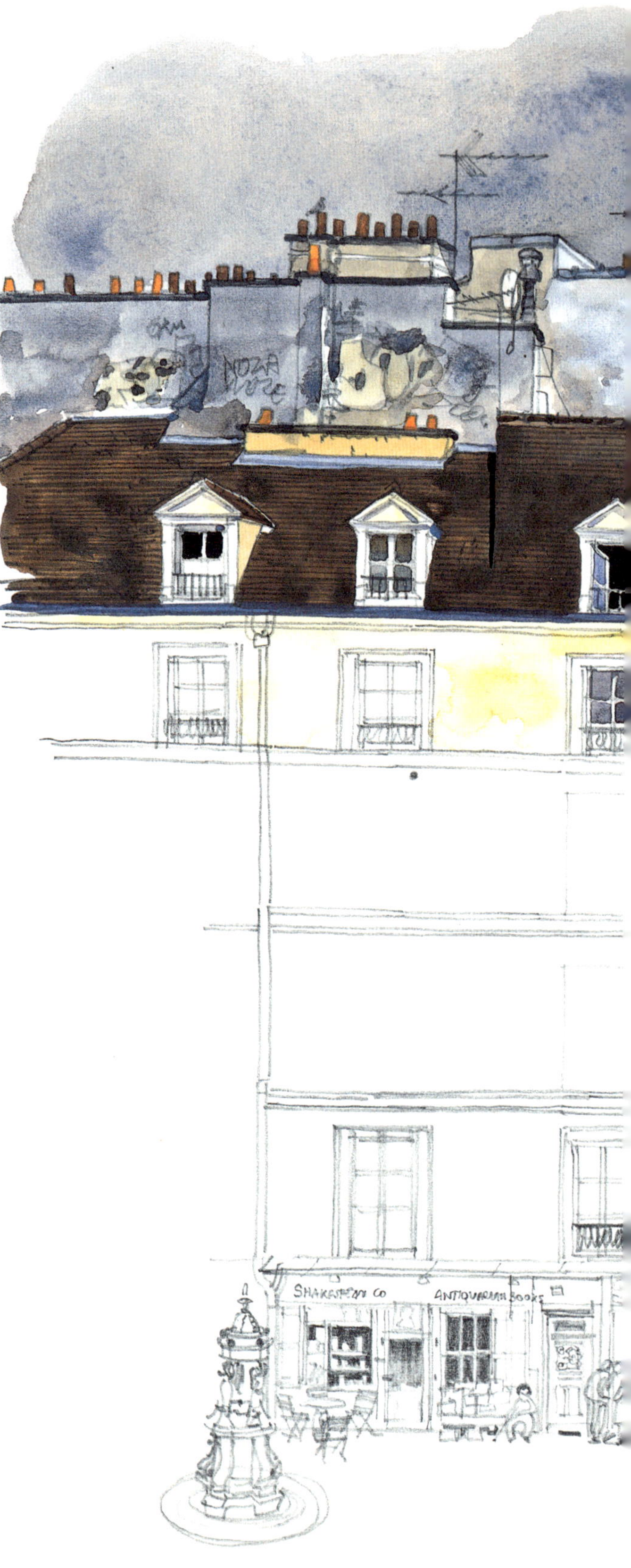

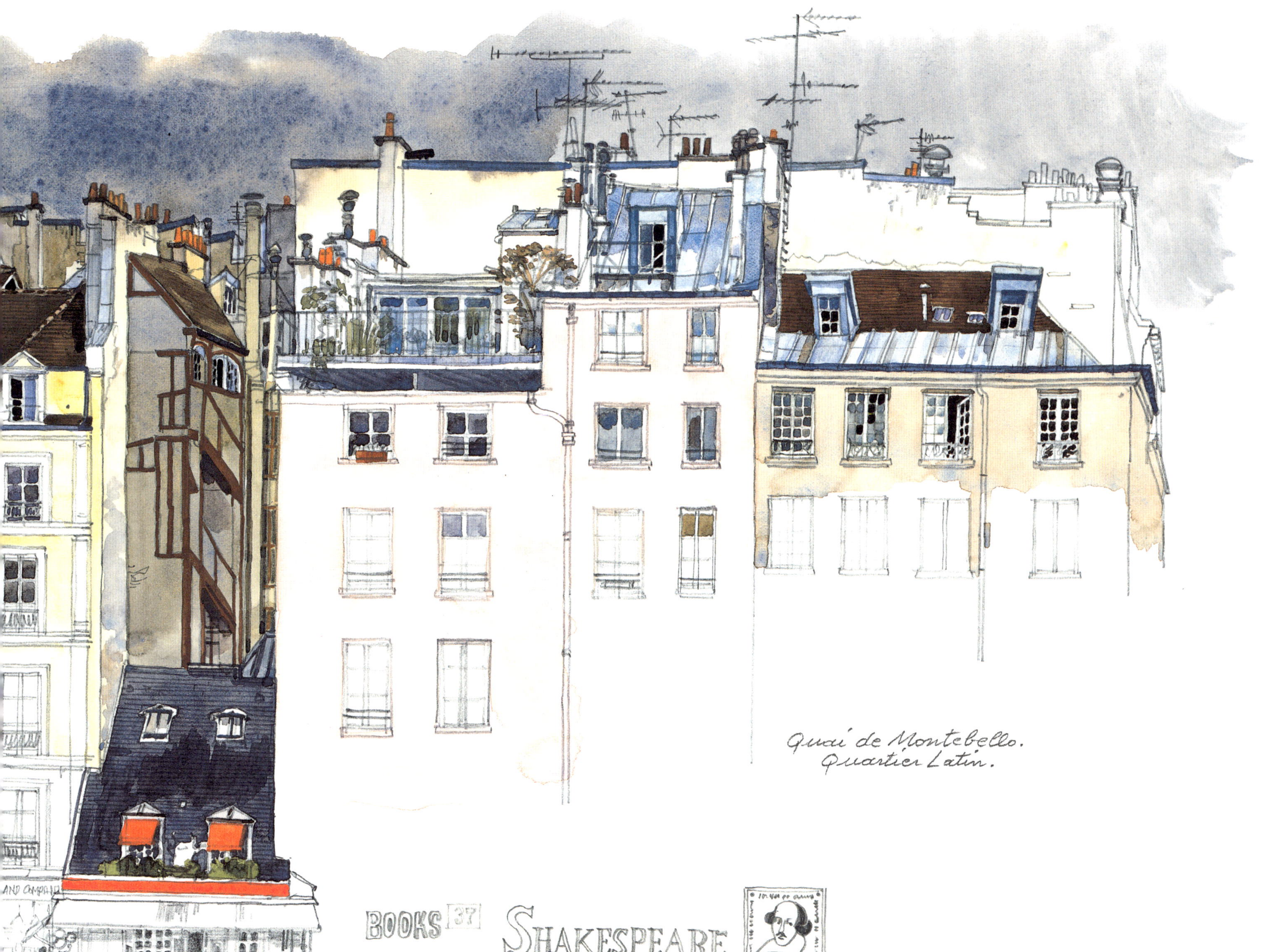

Quai de Montebello.
Quartier Latin.
BOOKS 37 SHAKESPEARE
AND COMPANY

Between snowflakes and iguanodons

Who is that wandering about on the roof of the Galerie de Paléontologie, between pigeons and iguanodons? A reckless scientist, a stealer of bones, a park keeper or just a lover of heights? Paris is under snow, but that weighs little upon his dreams. Spring is hidden, glistening, but he keeps walking. Down below, umbrellas tell the story of Paris. Just one plop, and the flakes turn to a little spray of water. Sadness is in the streets, on wet coats already thawing, or in the gutters. But where is this unknown man, in search of a fall? The long stretch of white in front of him is like a gentle song to his eye. He seems to be one sky ahead of us, a finger dipped into the universe, as if tasting cream. Down below, in a gallery of the museum, among the whale bones, time stands still.

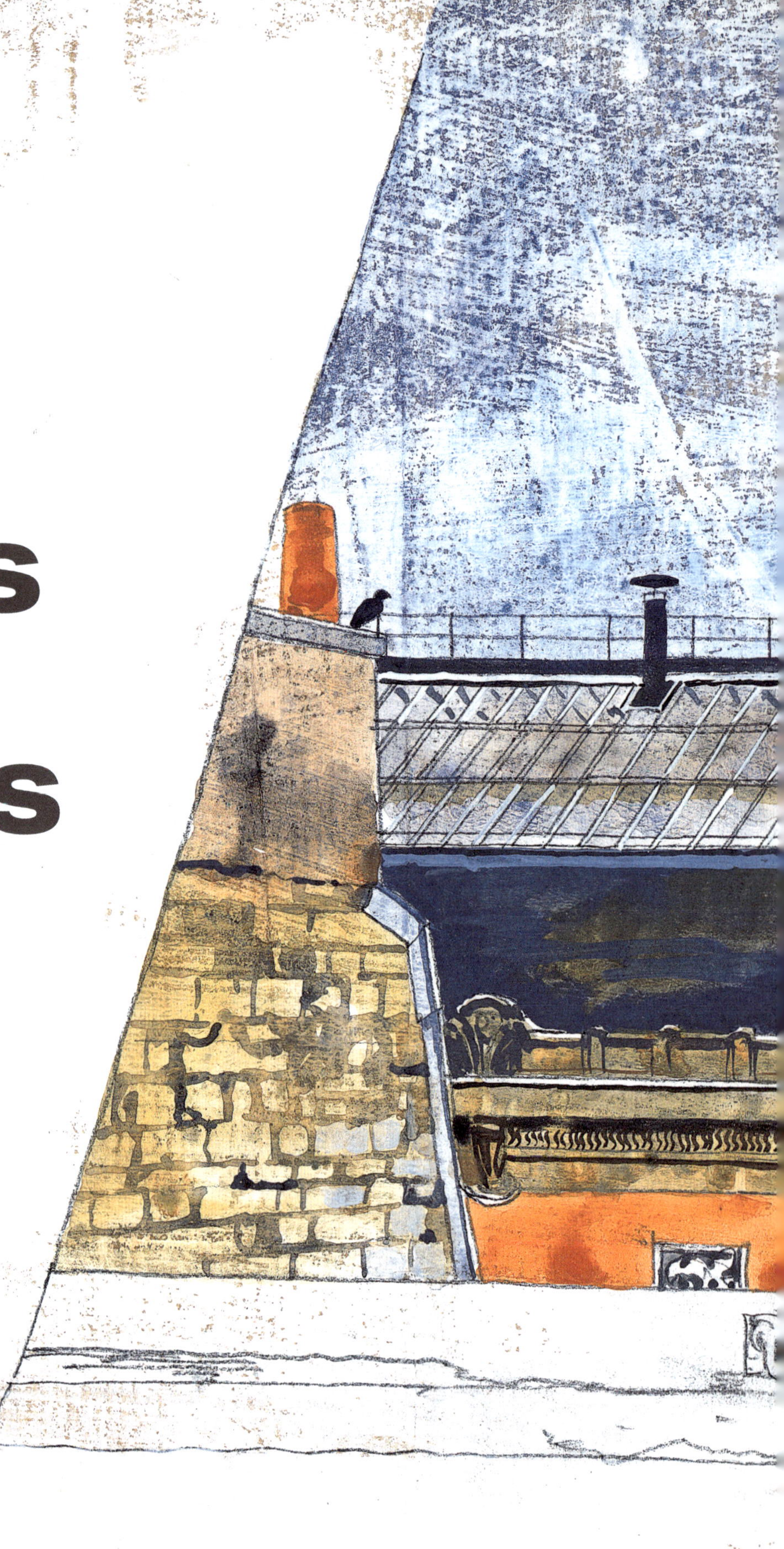

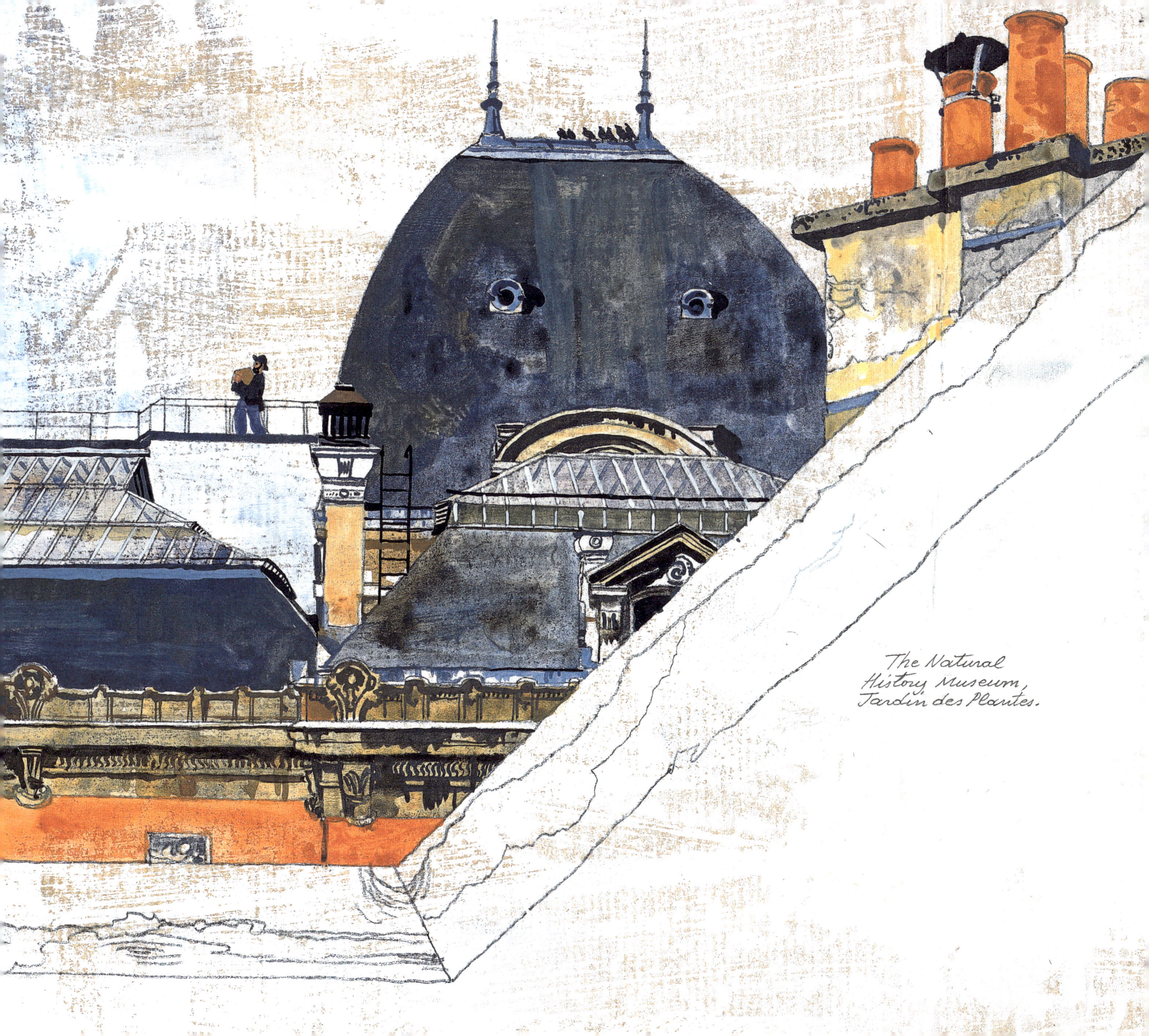
The Natural
History Museum,
Jardin des Plantes.

Don't leave anything on the train

The north wind has arrived. People huddle in their homes. Winter weighs heavily as night draws to a close. There's a chill in the air; the wind is penetrating, swirling under hats, through cracks in gutters and through windows that don't quite shut. Indoors, the café is enveloped in a misty halo, it's beginning to warm up. There's new light under the roofs, the hope for something brighter, a thought that can drive back the clouds, of trips to southern climes in November. But the north wind has definitely arrived to chill the cheeks of Paris, as if coming off the sea, blowing across the great glass roof as the city sleeps. A whole world is about to come to life with the first train, here in the Gare d'Austerlitz where everything is still, except for some people delivering bread, travellers having their first cigarette of the day, and dawn revellers reluctant to leave.

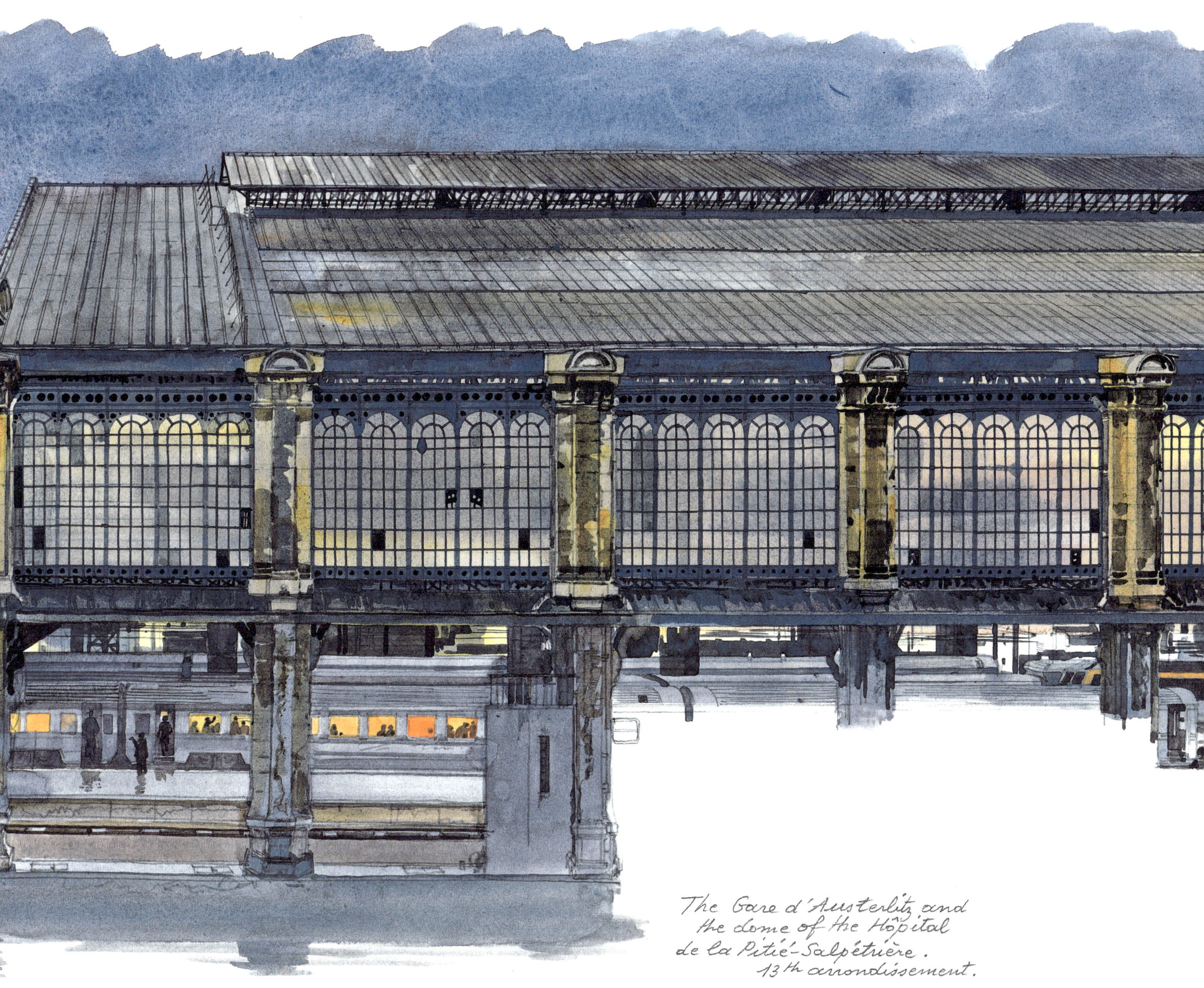

The Gare d'Austerlitz and
the dome of the Hôpital
de la Pitié-Salpêtrière.
13th arrondissement.

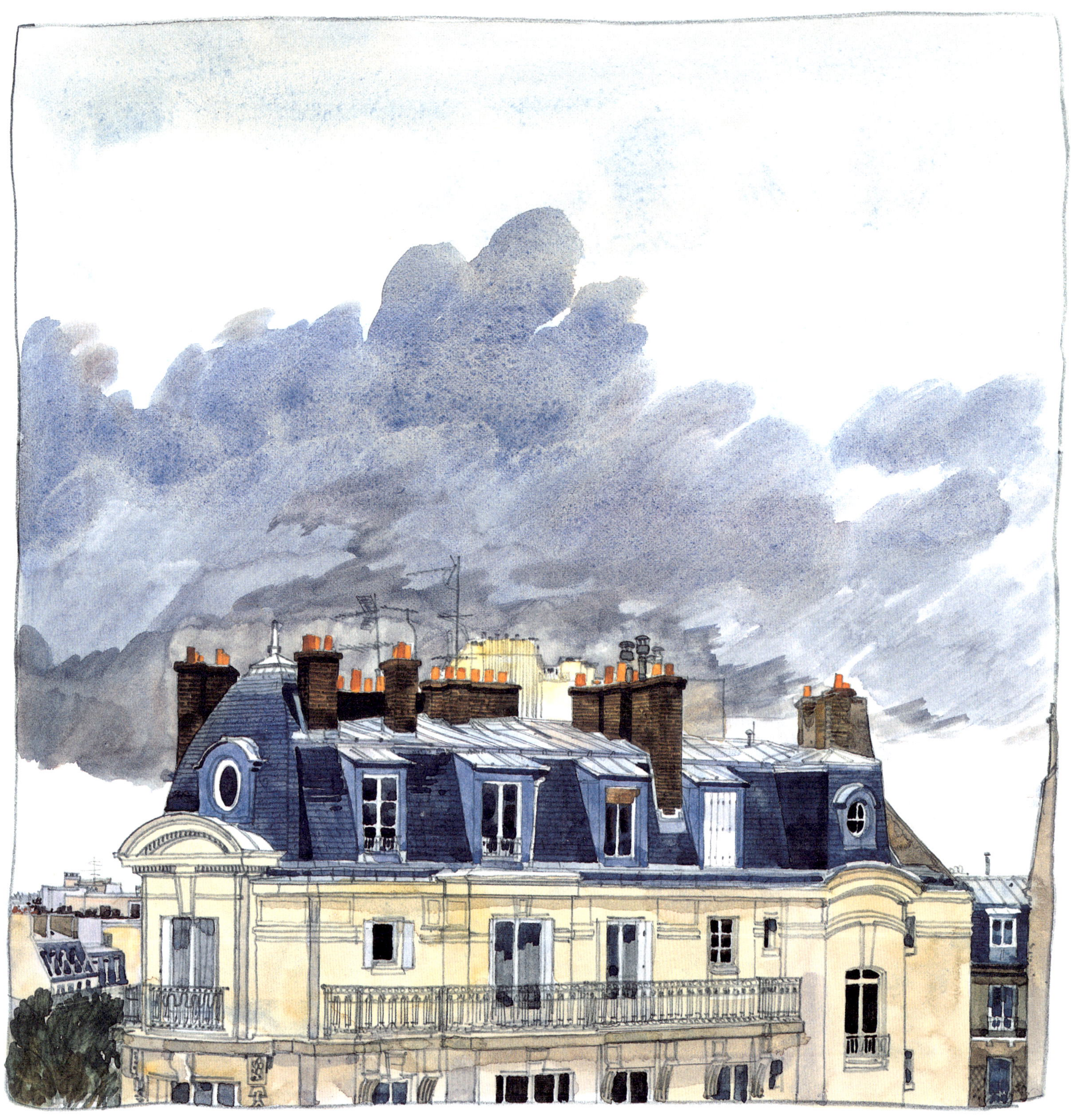

Avenue
du Géneral
Leclerc.
Alésia.

All aboard

You thread words onto the string of thoughts, a few glass beads to peer into the distance and see how Paris dances to the rhythm of the rooftops. A cloudscape or two pass by. Every moment is a step. From above, the crowd seems far away, a distant refrain that is heard but barely registered by the eye focused on the spirit of the heavens.

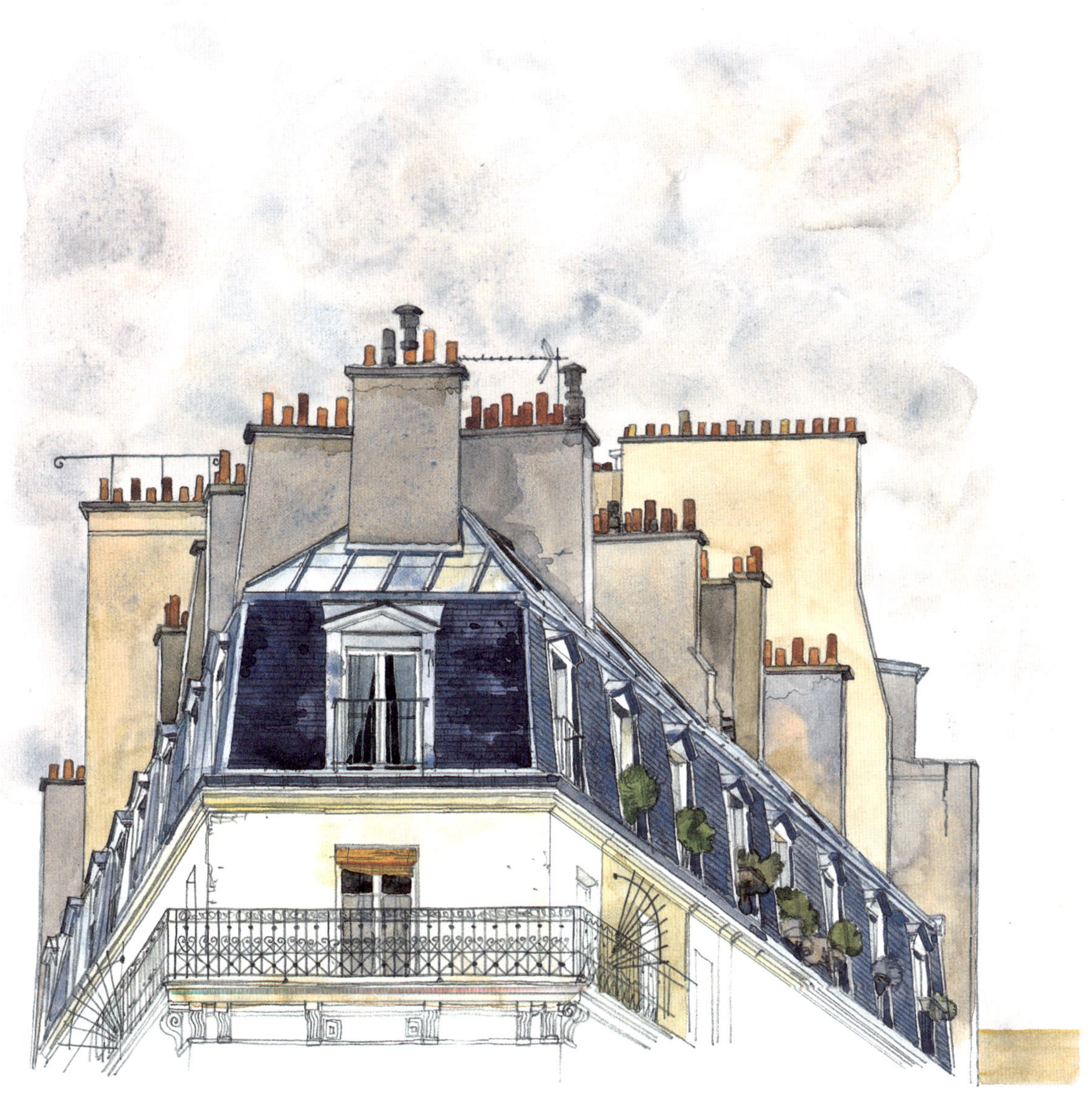

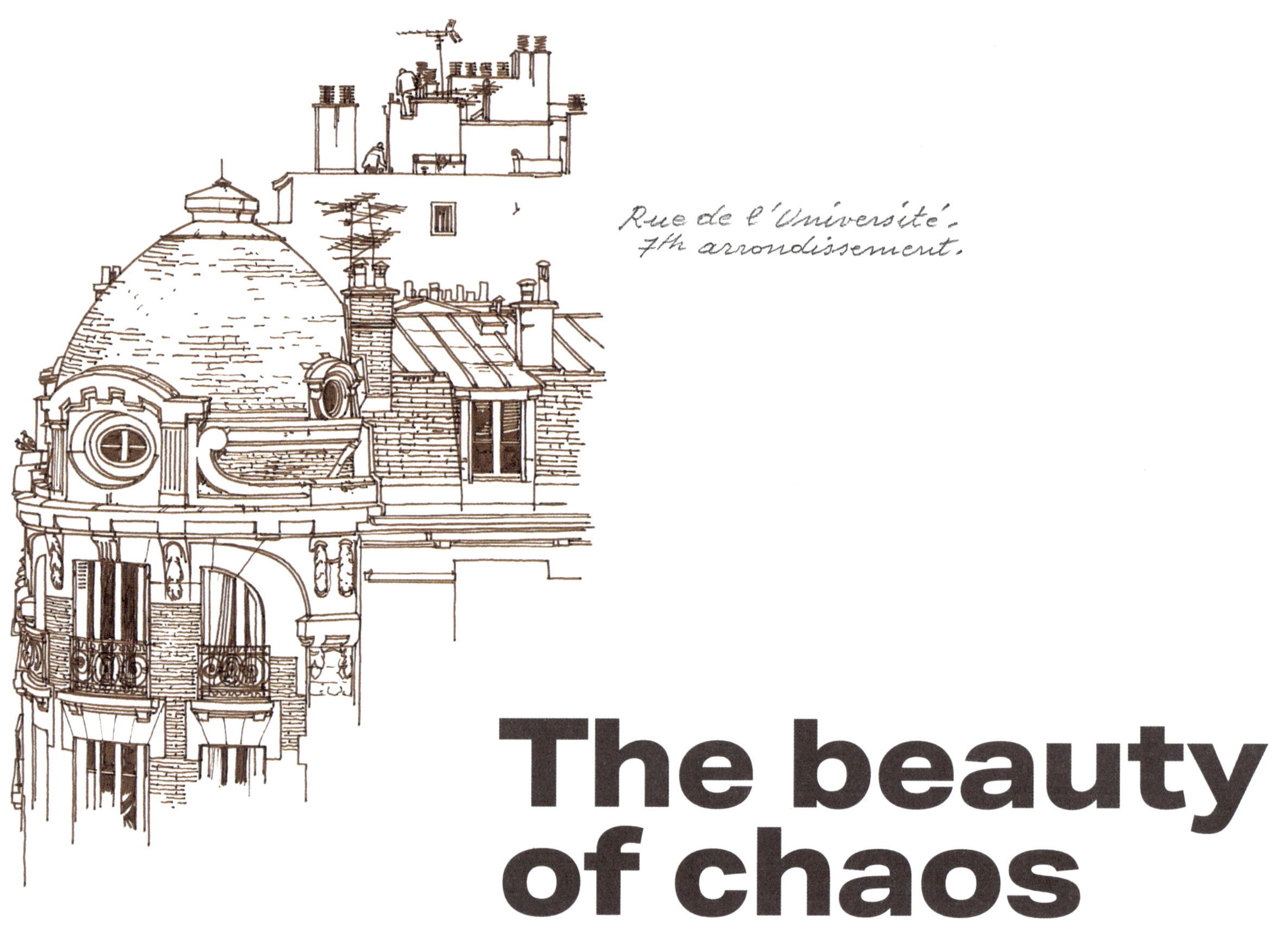

The beauty of chaos

In Paris, the roof is the city's least Cartesian aspect. A welter of materials, a desire to leave one's mark under the open sky: spike, cupola, dome, vertical line, a shape like an ammunition shell, a glass roof singing in the rain – we are in a tangled, overlapping unknown. Painters have felt the exuberance of a hidden Orient up there, or a sense of chaos, but nothing is more Parisian than this determination to make a world in one's own image, of choosing to be one's own self, and of holding on to that until the next world.

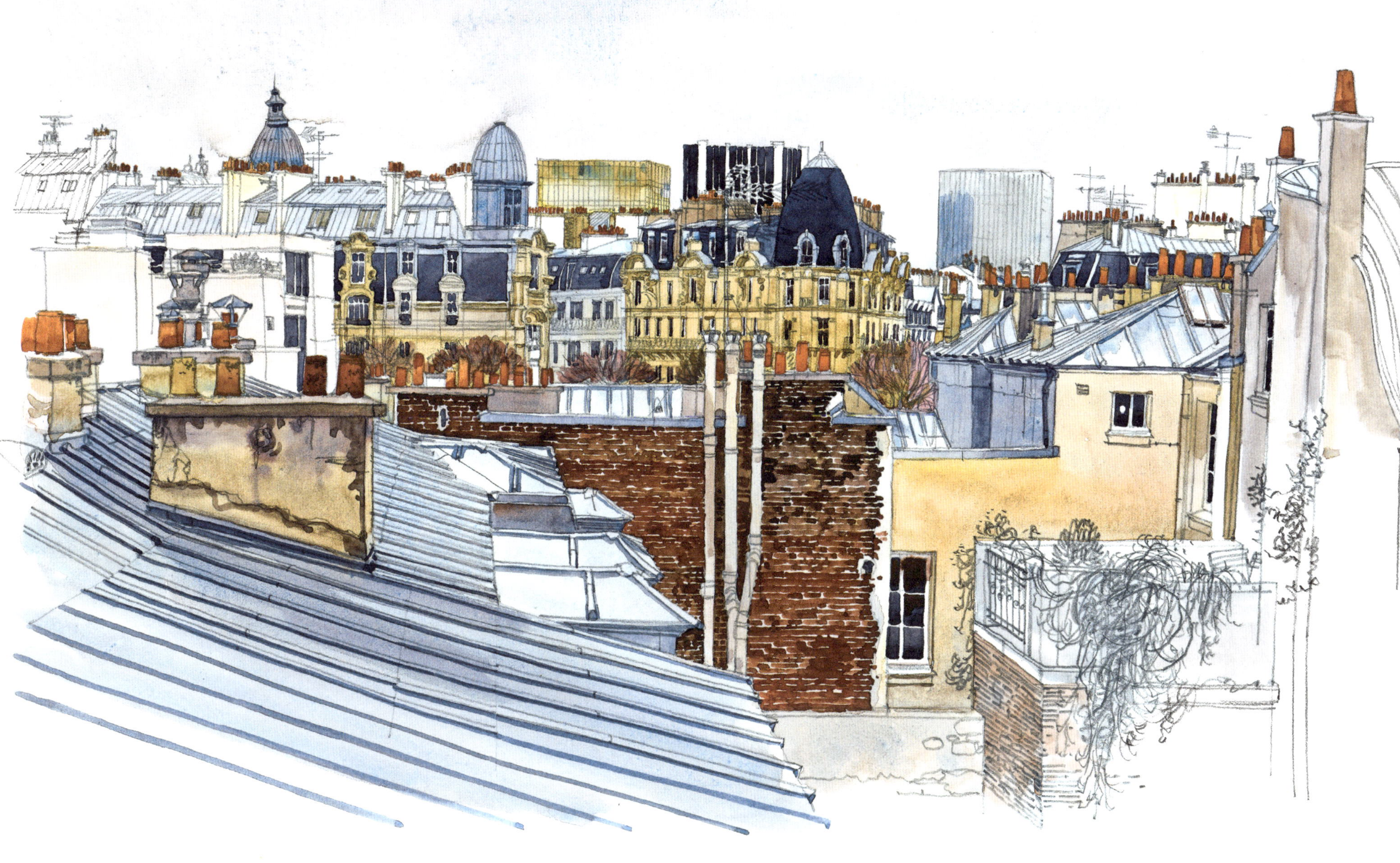

Rue de Charenton.
12th arrondissement.

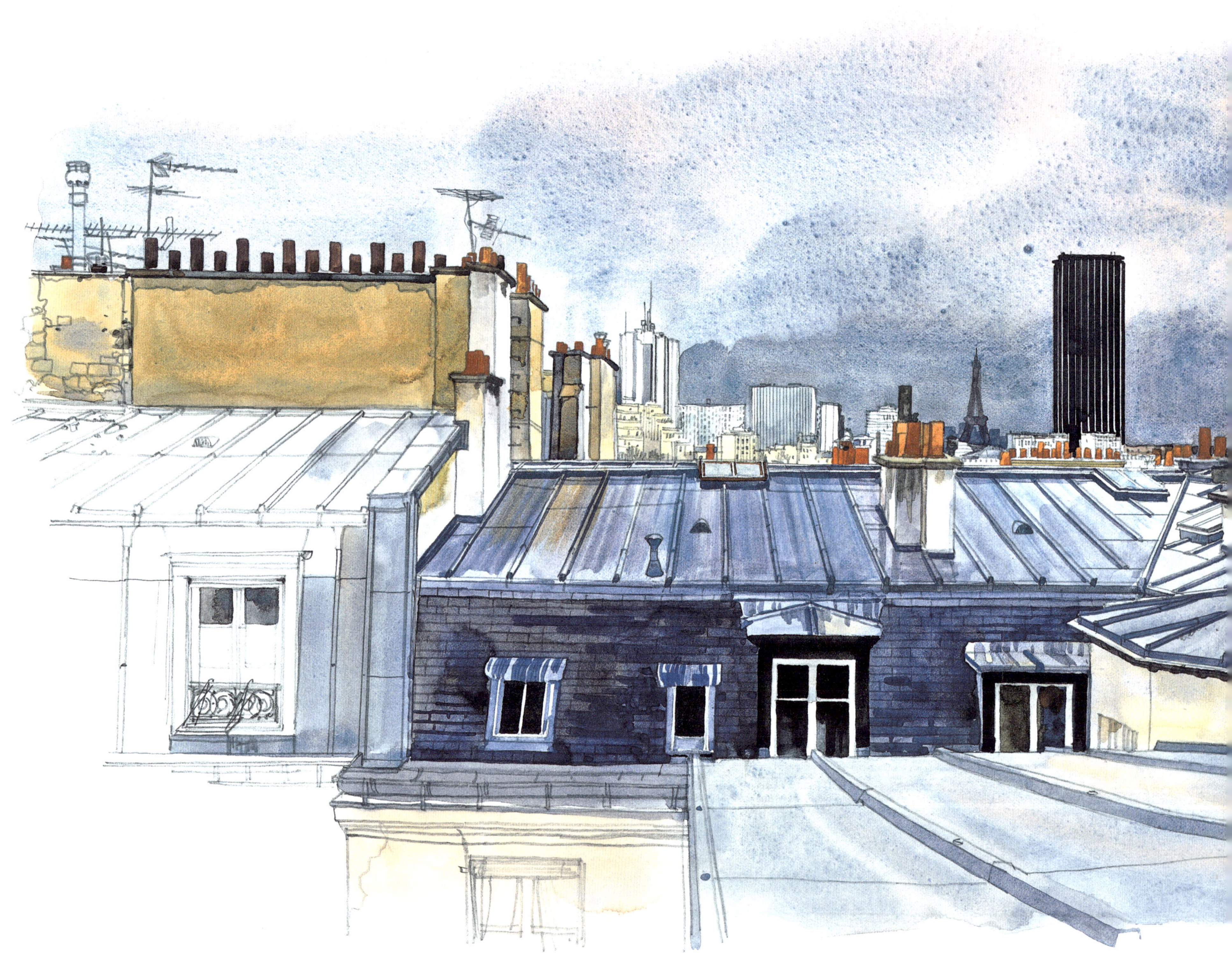

Dear neighbour

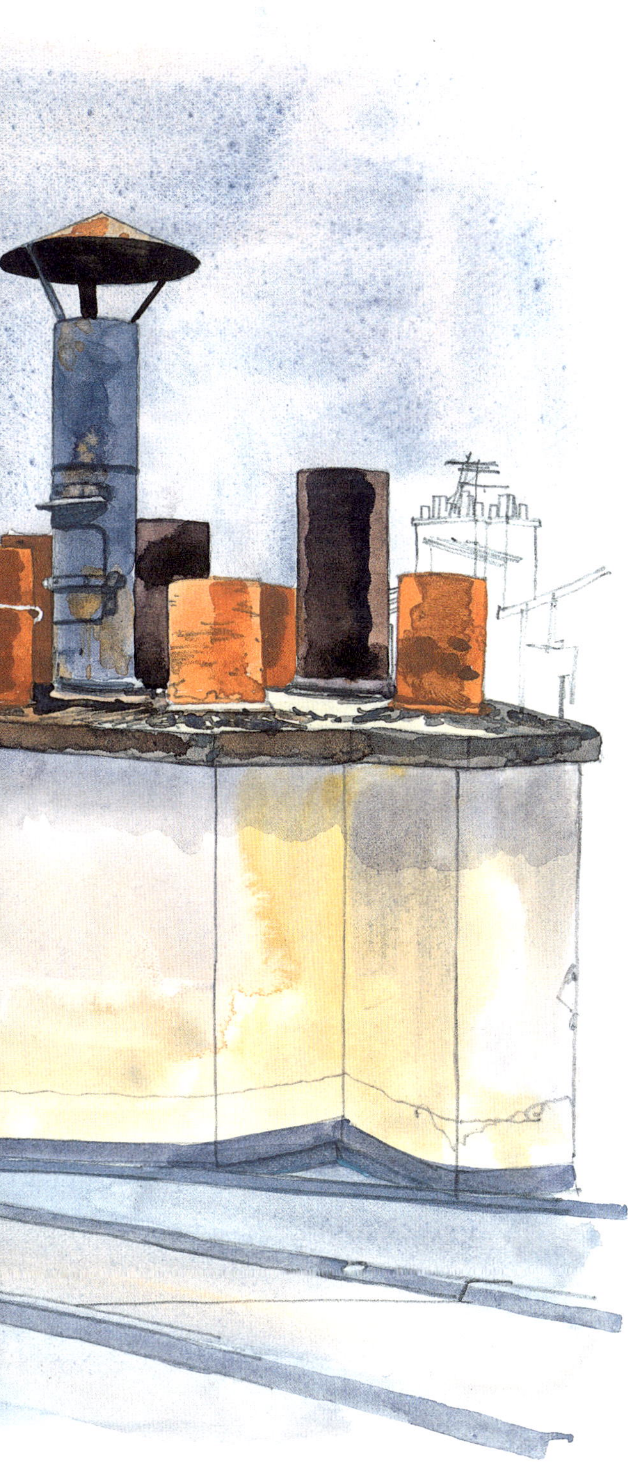

Hello there, I'm looking at you for a chat. Eyes talk, so do arms, crossing and uncrossing, moving a little or slightly askance, talking casually. Not prosperous, but close to the sky, like you. Have you seen the drizzle, dear neighbour? That mischievous cat? Your aerial is twisted. Does that matter? What do you do for a living? Who are you, under your roof? I'm sending you a sign, but can you see this wink from where you are, from where you hang your hat? Life is beautiful, somewhat precarious in another language, that's what I wanted to say. Good morning and good evening, see you tomorrow, maybe never, dear neighbour from the other shore, from the other skylight. It's going to rain, but it's Sunday after all, time to let your eyes wander, far from words that weigh down conversations.

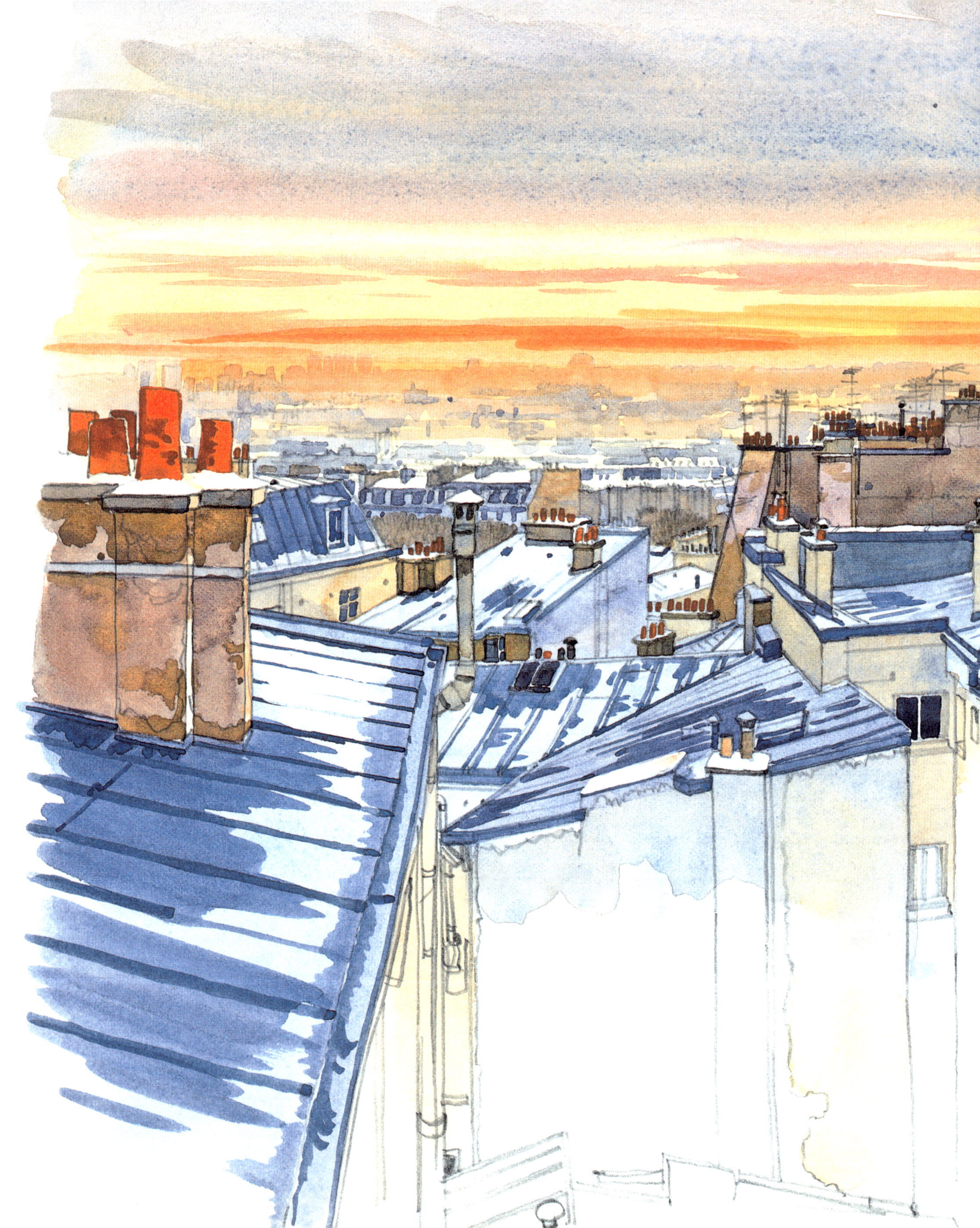

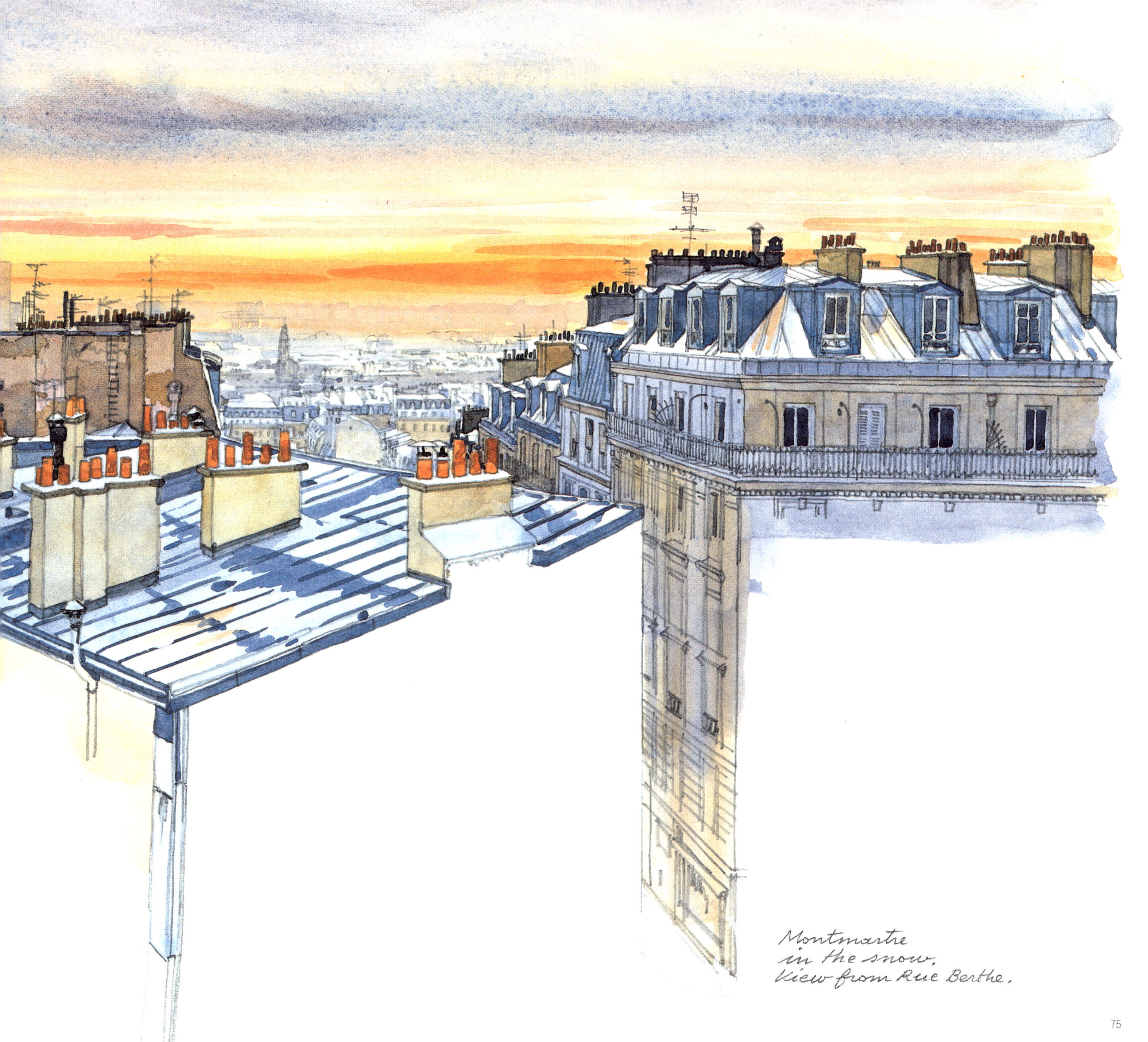

Montmartre
in the snow.
View from Rue Berthe.

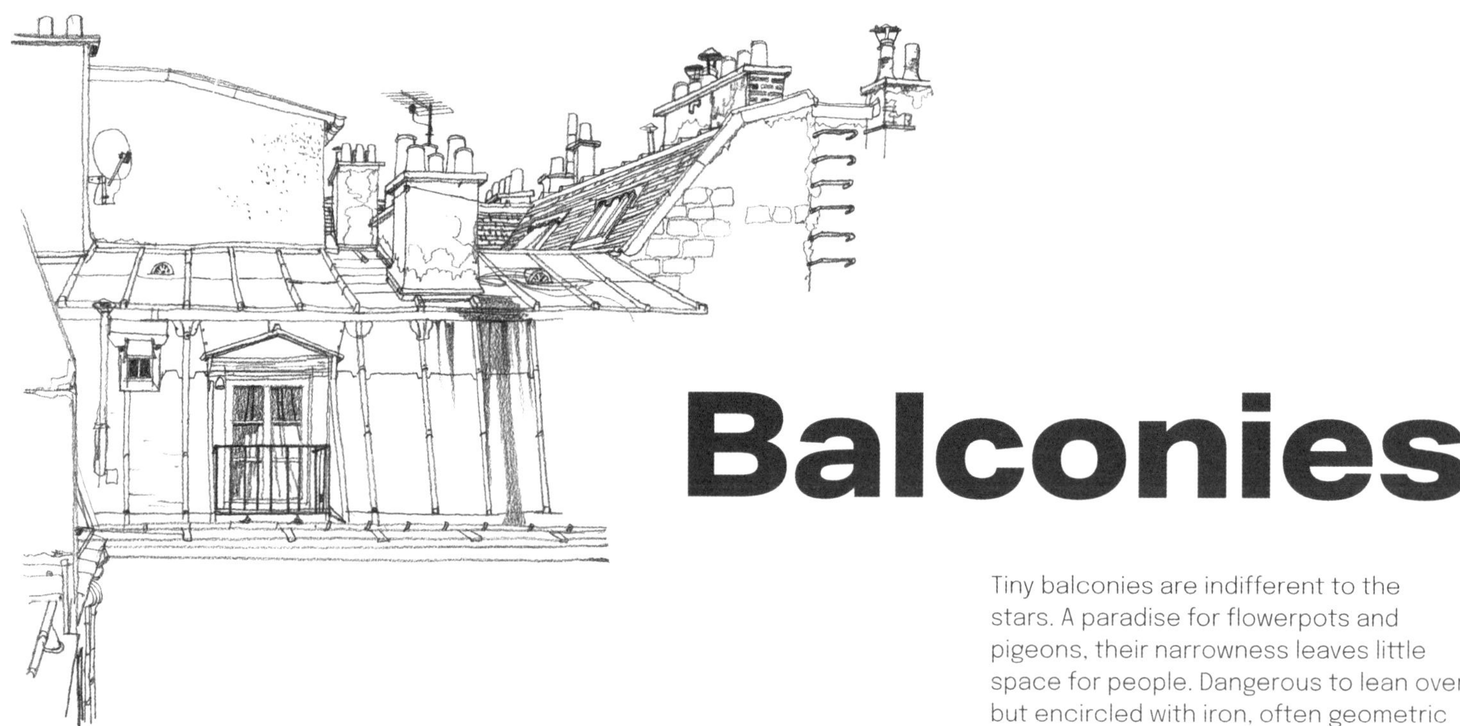

Balconies

Tiny balconies are indifferent to the stars. A paradise for flowerpots and pigeons, their narrowness leaves little space for people. Dangerous to lean over, but encircled with iron, often geometric or forming decorative motifs, they sit up there in state with a kind of false humility. They reflect the sun in all kinds of ways, an echo of times past under slanting beams of light. They rise in tiers to the rhythm of the façades, accompanying and punctuating windows that interlock with each other, repeating themselves like portholes on an ocean liner. These little balconies don't gape open-mouthed at the sky, a vastness that to them seems too featureless. They are tiny spaces, places to accommodate our dreams.

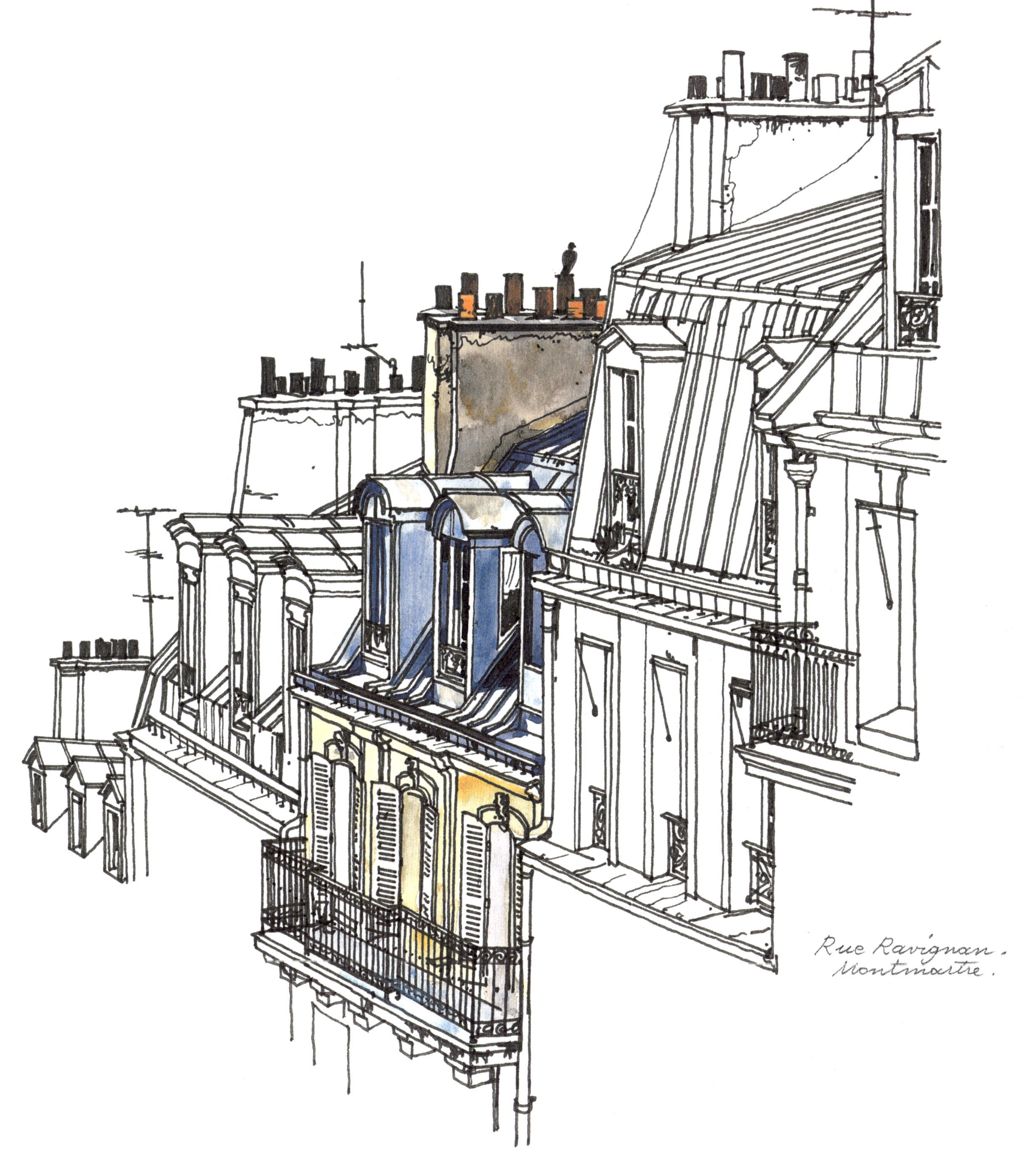

Rue Ravignan.
Montmartre.

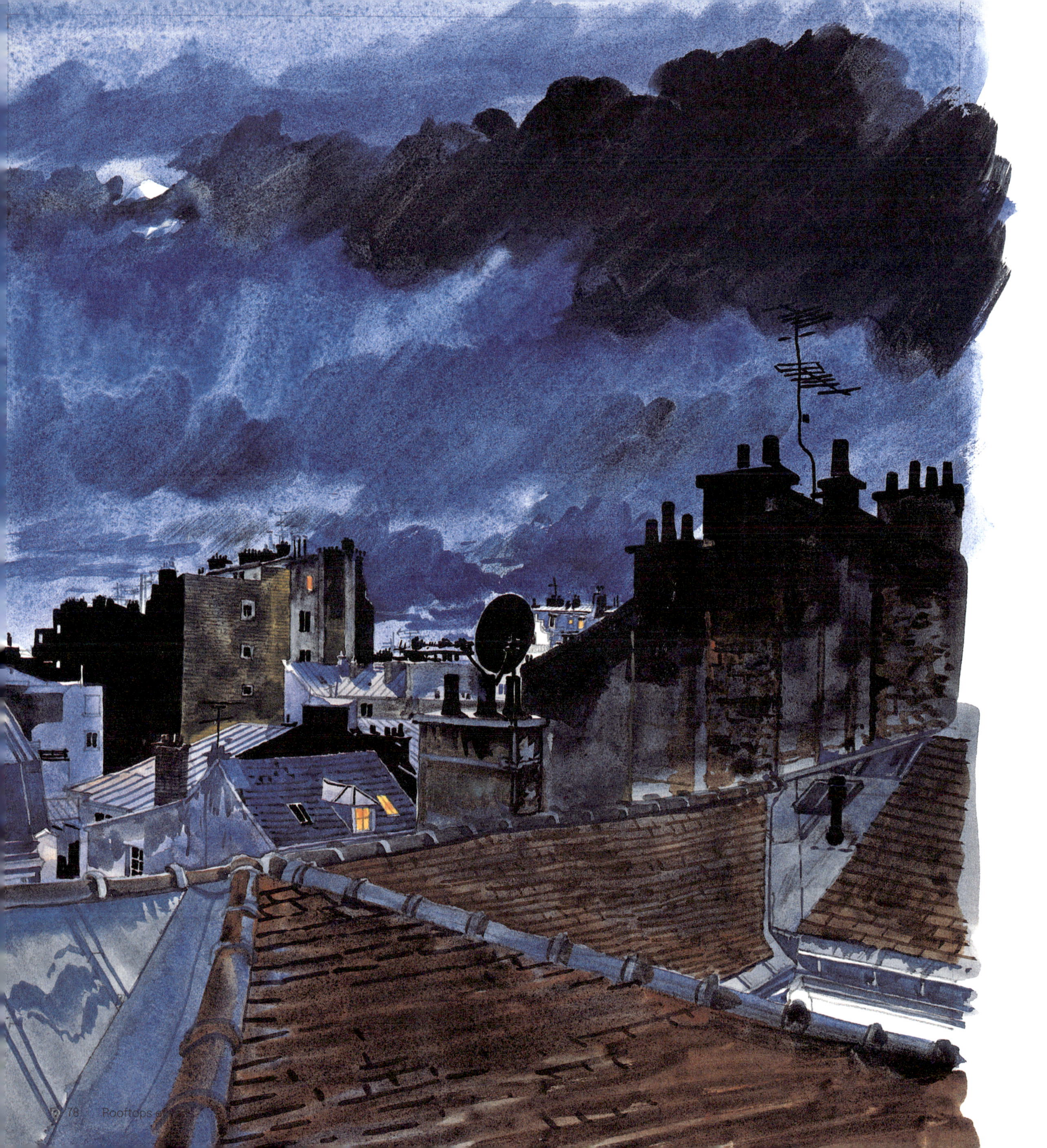

78   Rooftops of

Night time in Ménilmontant

Night grows pale at the window. Ménilmontant grows quiet. Several lights seem to be dozing off, but still keep watch: beacons where shadows slip by, without need of the moon. Behind the glimmering lights, everyone has someone, something: an embrace, the weather forecast, a soap opera. Sometimes a curtain bangs like a door, a cat sharpens its claws, the clock ticks on. A small world unfolds along the thread of time while the sky takes on bolder, electric blues, demanding a more direct look.

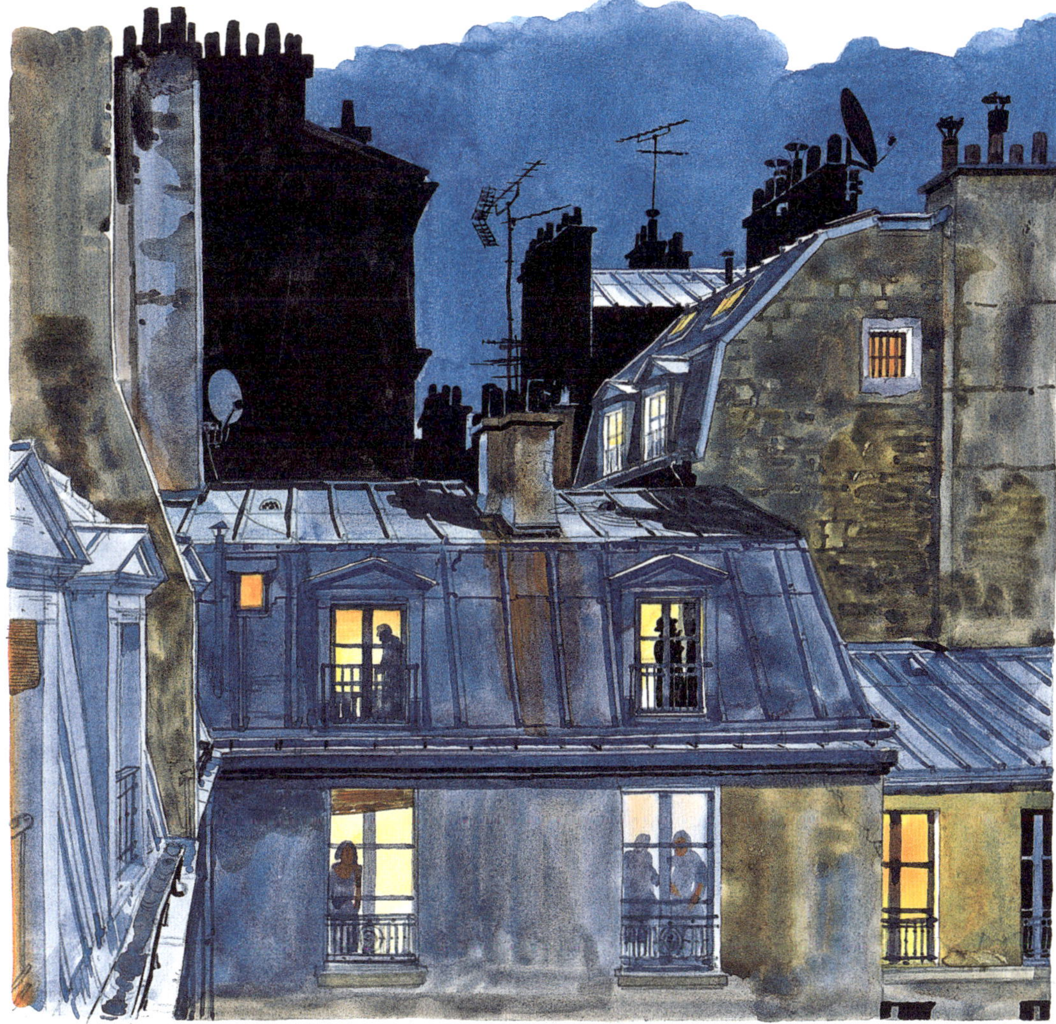

The first aerial photograph

Paris fills your eyes. No need to move. The blue sky becomes a song. The roofs are perched like cats high up. The sky is a passer-by. Without a word, without a movement, Paris gives of itself. In Rue Saint-Eleuthère, in January, beauty works its way into the scene. A landscape of attic windows and chimneys opens up where each is special, without actually flying. It was on a day long ago, not far from the squares of Montmartre, from the Cimetière du Calvaire and the Wallace Fountain, that from a tethered balloon a dreamer by the name of Nadar took the world's first aerial photograph, rising up in the air to allow Paris really to fill his eyes.

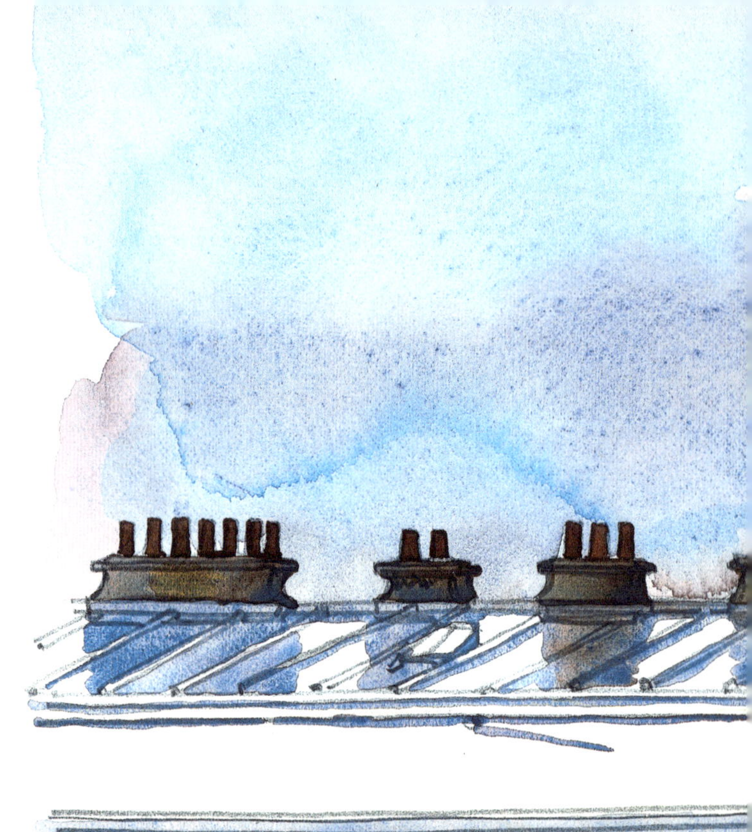

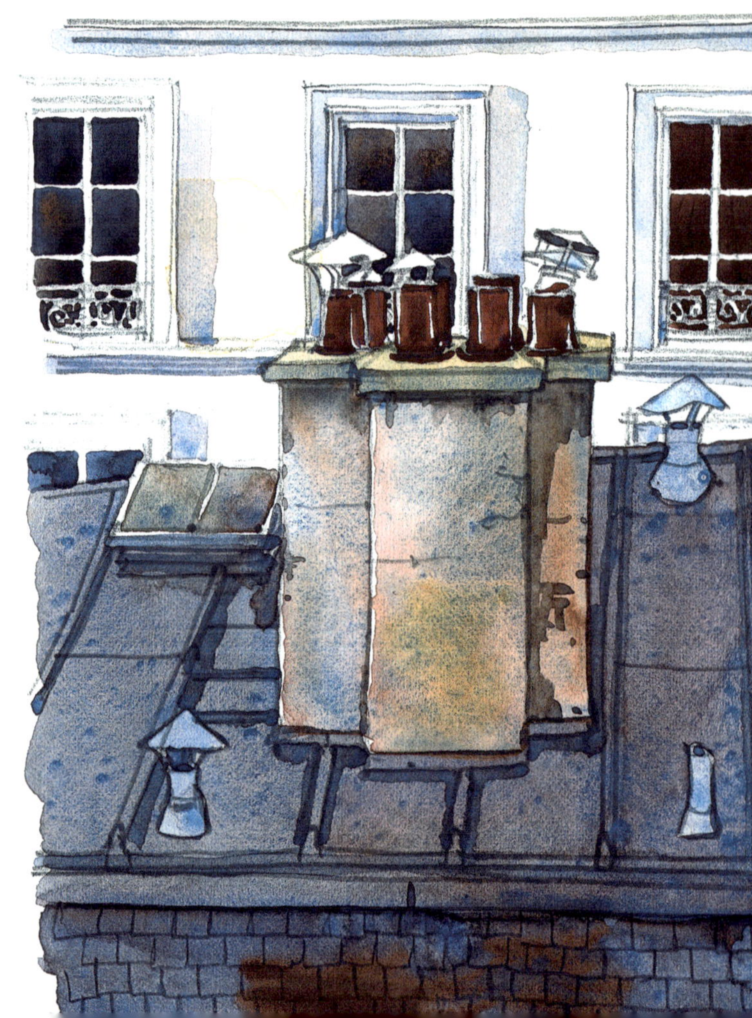

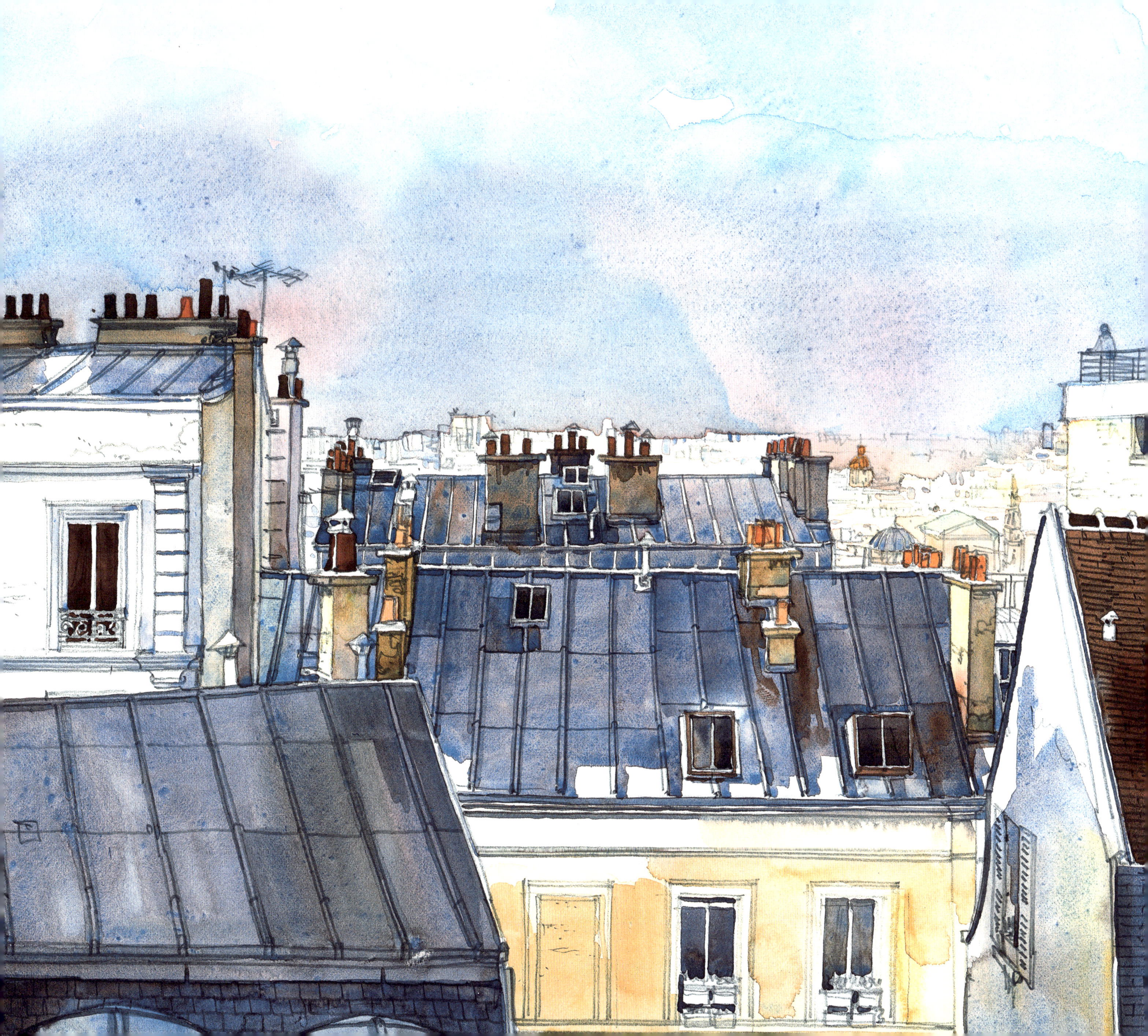

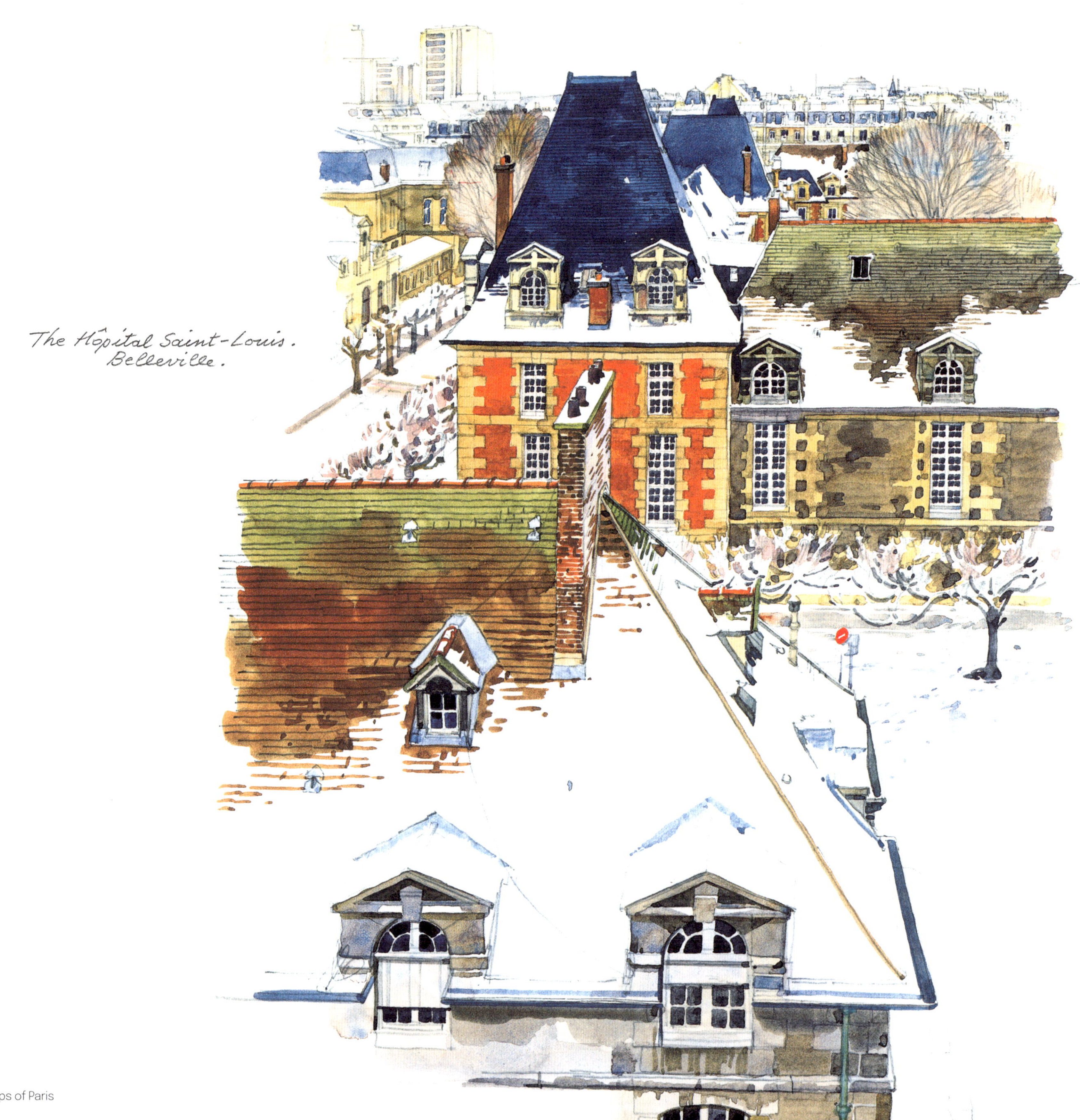

The Hôpital Saint-Louis.
Belleville.

The patience of snow

Here we must speak of the patience of snow. Of its jazz-like quality as it falls, improvising, of its indistinct voice as it lingers, hesitating before settling. But also of its wisdom, that can be seen by anyone who slows down. It gently covers; it does not decorate. It follows the waves of corrugated iron sheets. Today, this talent for contemplation is shown up in the grounds of the Hôpital Saint-Louis, reminding us of fields of old, of that century of plague, of nursing-home wards with ceilings high as a church, of that place of healing, of contagion too, where, to escape fate, eyes lifted to the glass roof, you had to recite your "Quis contra Deum, sine Deus ipse". Nowadays, the snow is left to its own thoughts, untouched by angels' feet. Once upon a time, nurses in white used to come and collect it up. The architects had made provision for ventilation and lighting, but not for drinking water; snow had to be taken from the roofs, frozen or not, for the washerwomen and the laundry. How good it still is to contemplate the patience of the snow. It has always been there to allow men, thus calmed, to look a little more deeply into their hearts.

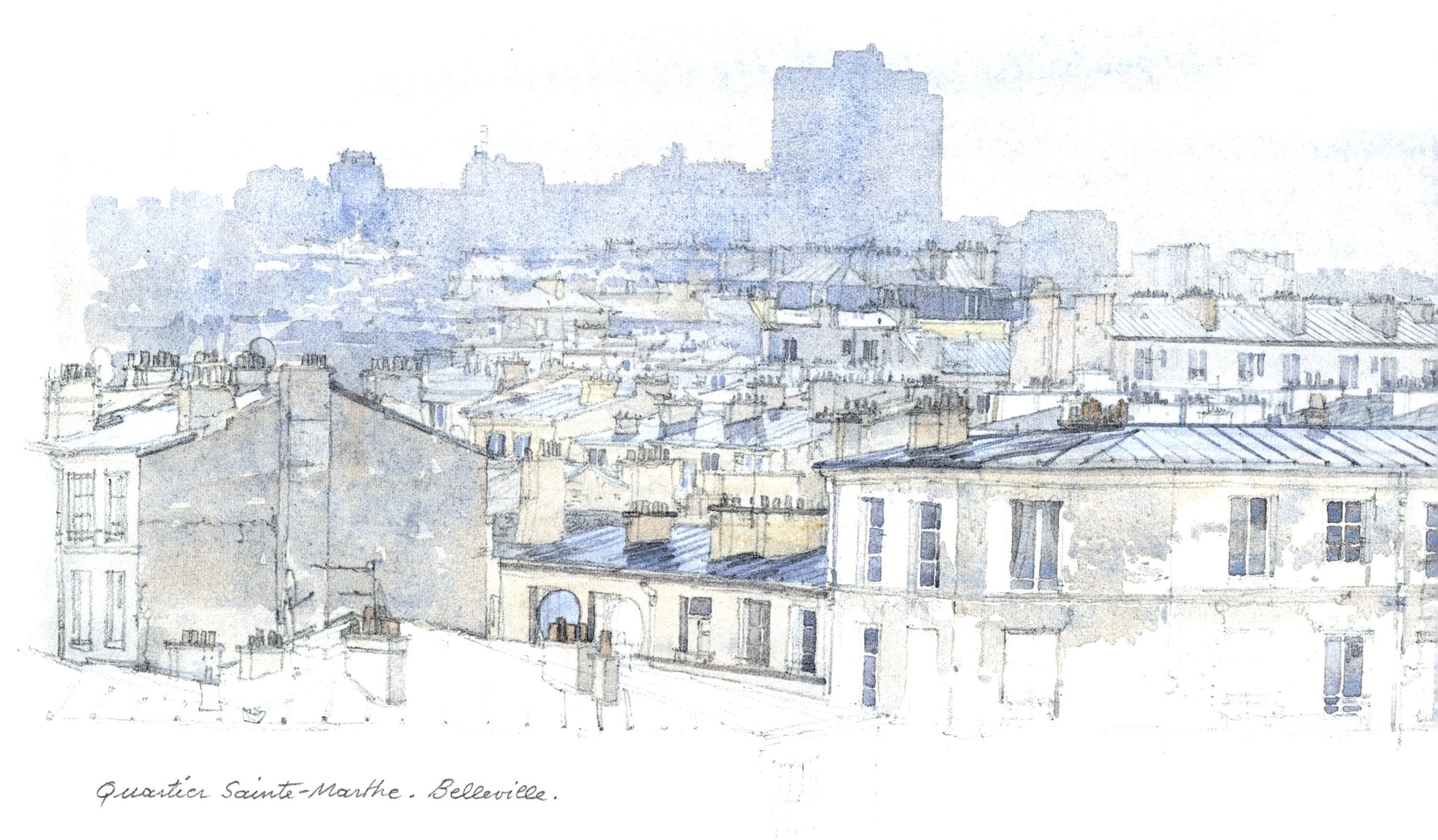

Quartier Sainte-Marthe . Belleville.

A misty dream

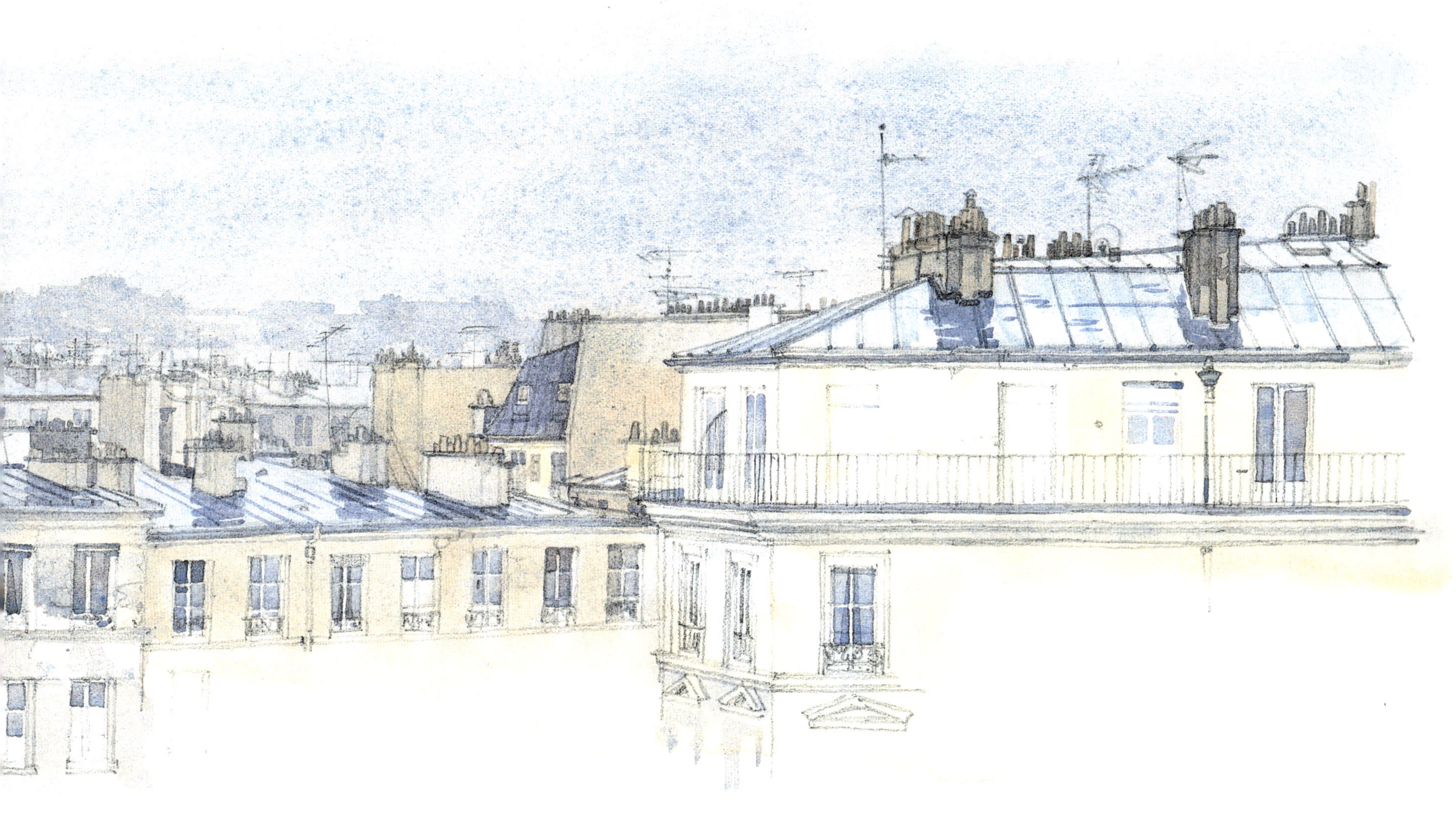

Roofs are not made for angels. Sometimes you discover your most earthly desires there. "If only we had a roof all of our own," say two lovers in passing. Imagine such a roof, there before any of the others existed, floating like some beauty seated in mid-air, with the promise that everything beneath would materialise even if a few low clouds or a mist over Belleville had to be dispelled first. Making your own roof just as you would make a nest, what a wonderful idea! To breathe with the bird that deigns to fly down. To forego all grandeur in order to focus on the most accessible cloud, the one that forms as a pair. To be free to move on, together with the other. To marry the skies and earthly places, sun and fog. To be roof or poem.

The other side of Paris

There are some holes in the city, patches of rust above eye level. Can you see them? To avoid upsetting the more elegant districts with its noxious fumes, industrial Paris lies to the east and north, its warehouses like chessboards with uniform black squares. This Paris is an affront to the city's leaded roofs, with violent transitions from one material to another. And there, other memories come flooding back, thoughts long-forgotten: images of caps and overalls, too-bulky sweaters and blunt talk. We tell ourselves that the roofs also bear the traces of hard work, of thoughts trying to escape from places too hot or too cold. There's history here, draining away, almost invisibly, through the rusty holes.

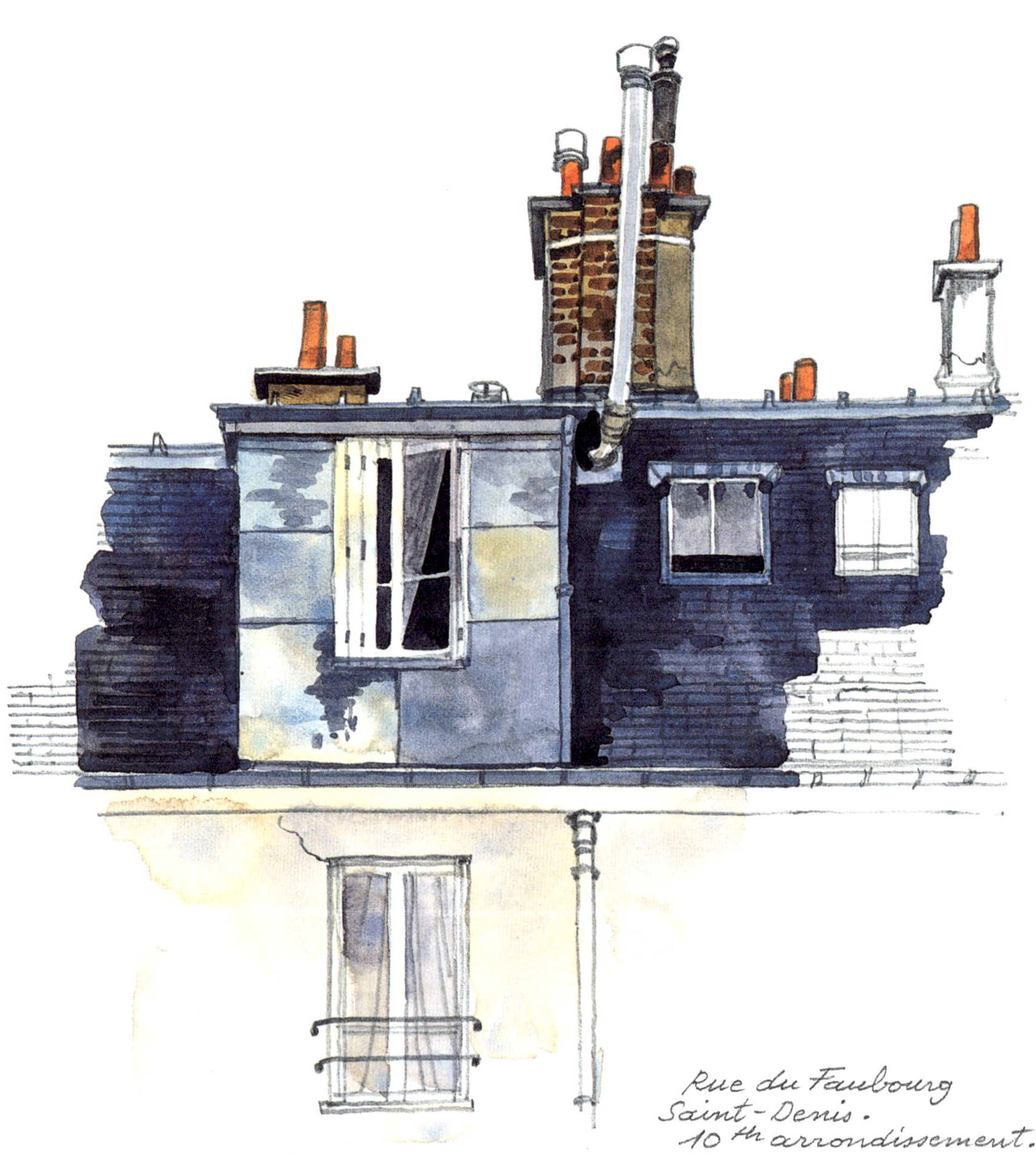

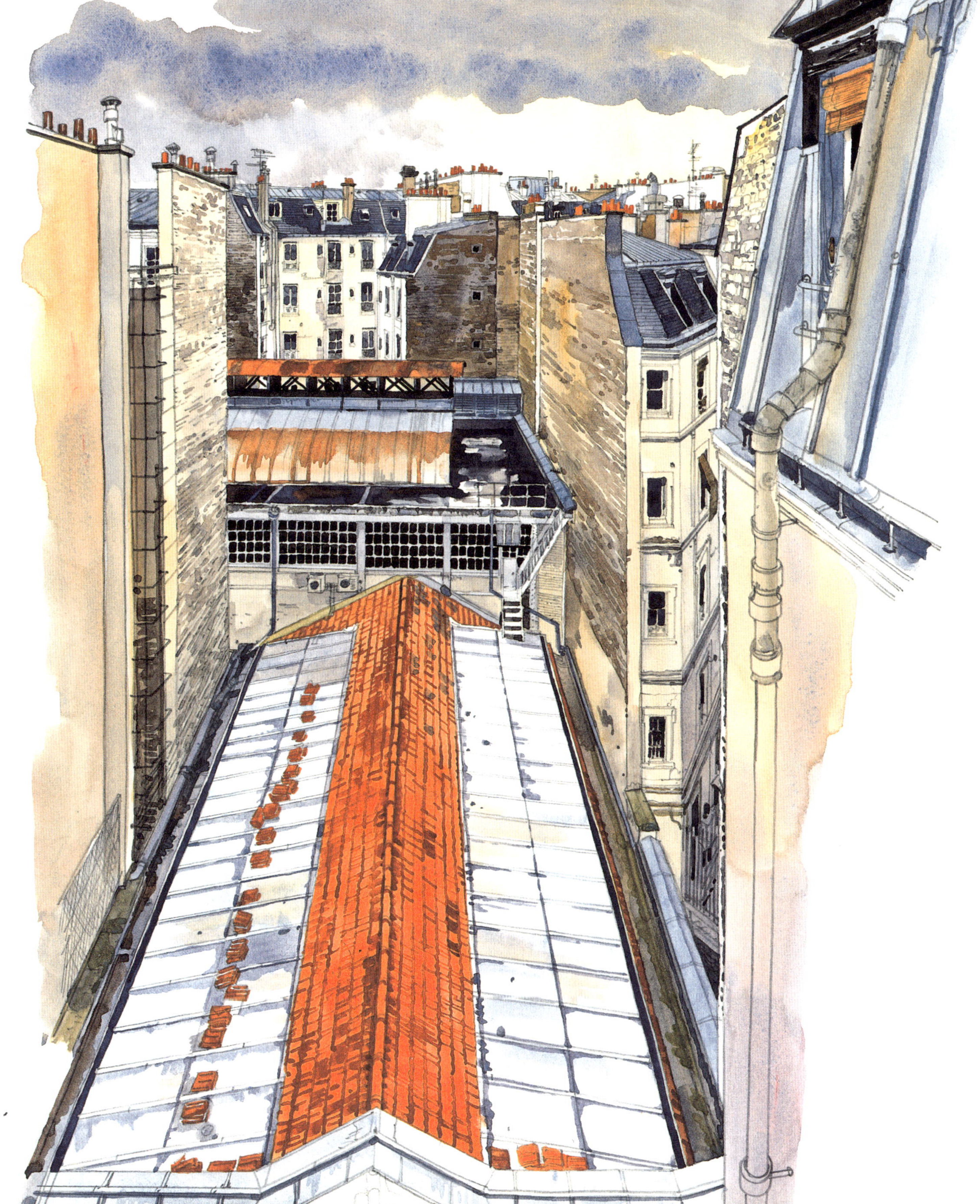

Avenue de
la République.
République.

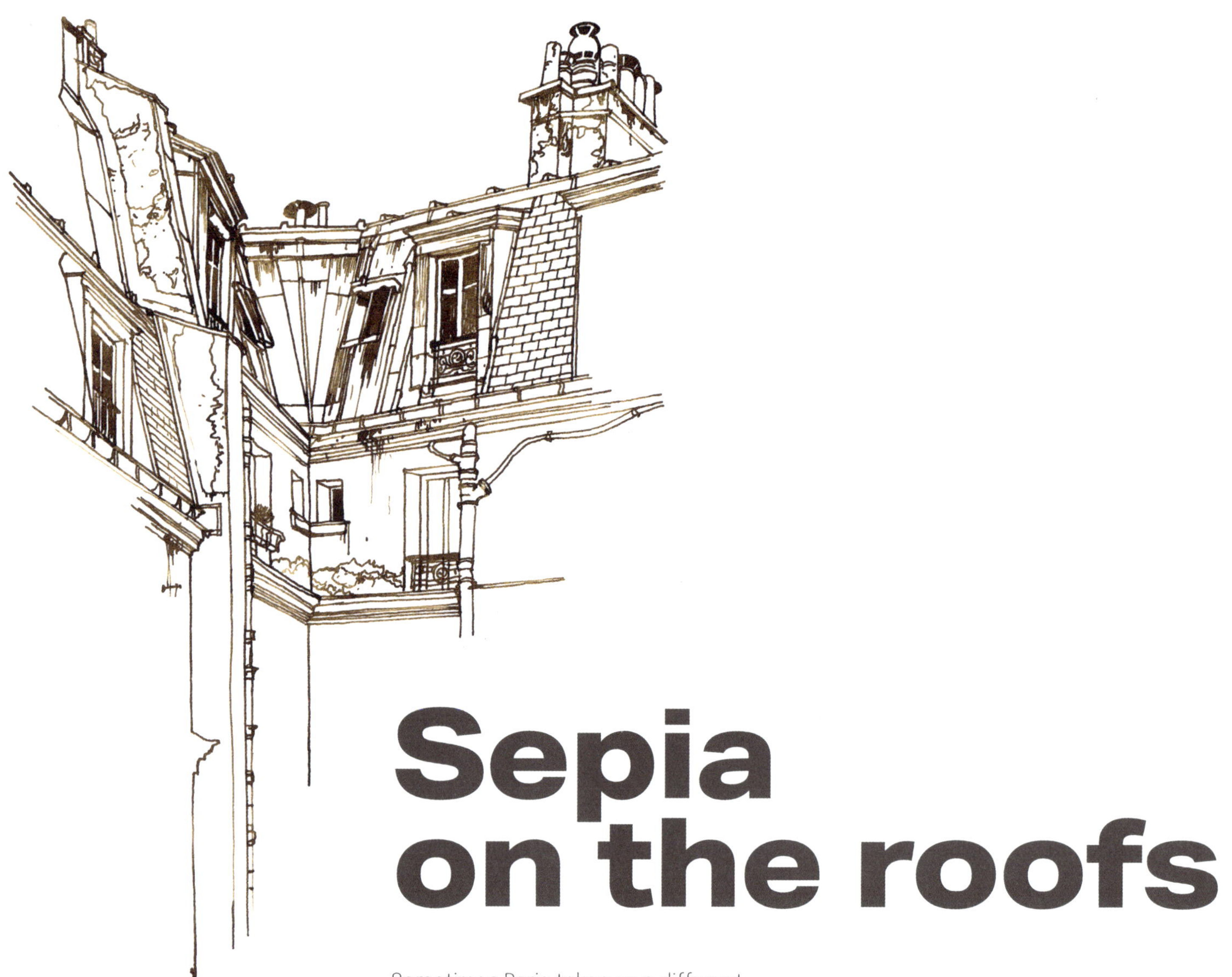

Sepia on the roofs

Sometimes Paris takes on a different look, as if in an old photograph. Rue de Belleville, now, fallen on hard times far from the golden days of old. Rue du Buisson-Saint-Louis and Rue de l'Atlas, too. A maze of backstreets giving a fluid effect, traces of light, of fleeting moments. Sometimes Paris looks different, far from the heavenly colonnades, nothing but a light sepia roof for decoration, bathed in a forgotten dish of silver nitrate.

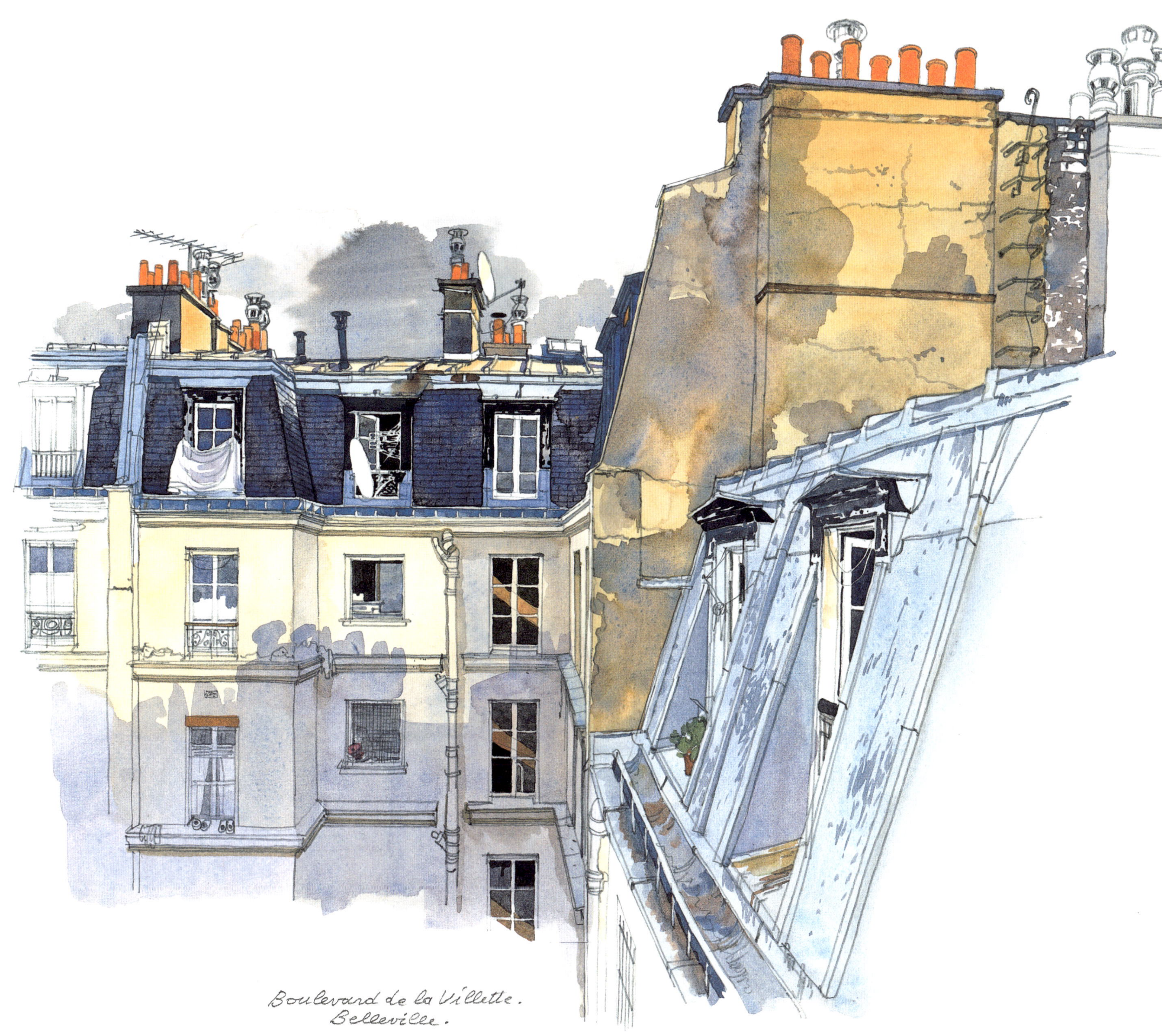

Boulevard de la Villette.
Belleville.

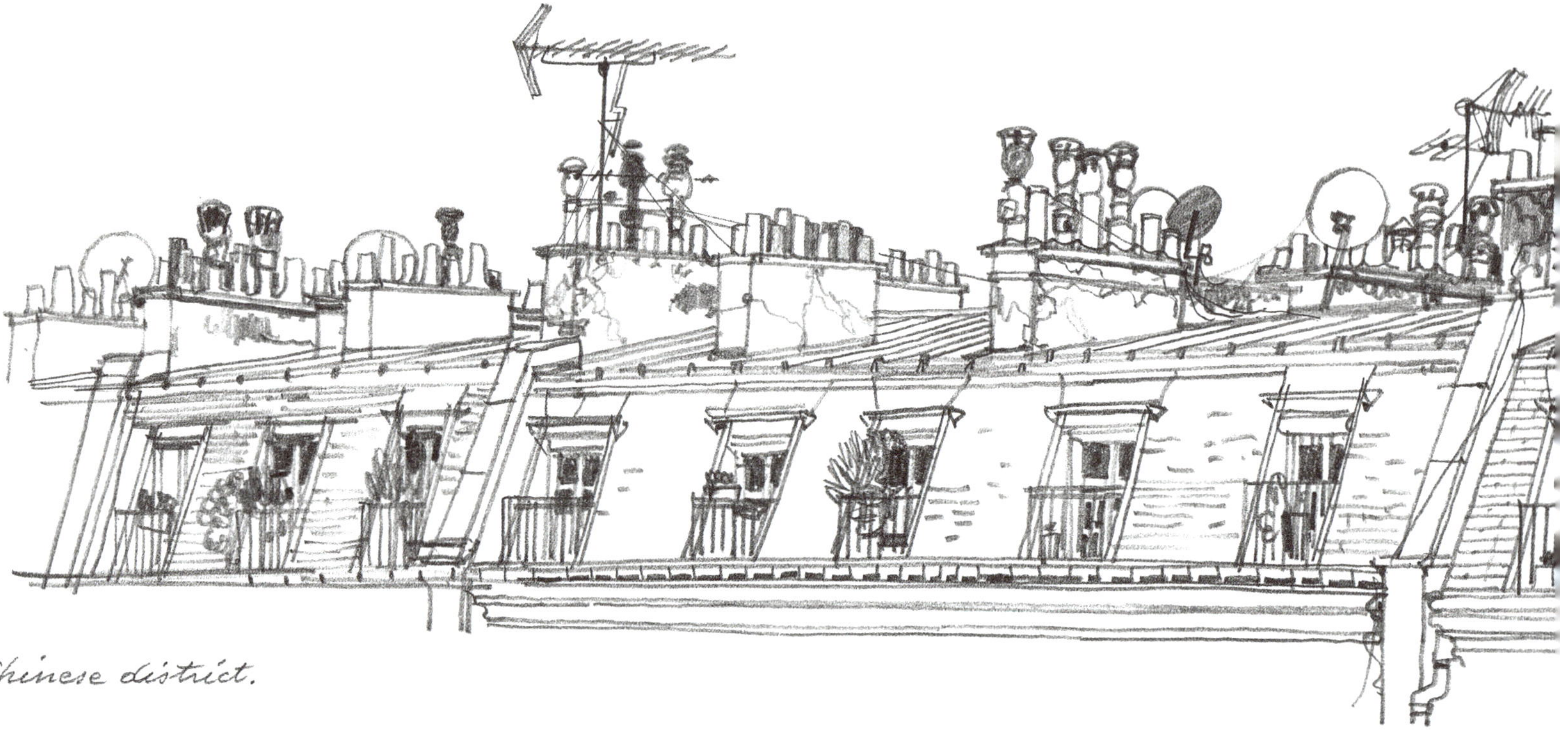

Rue Civiale.
Belleville's Chinese district.

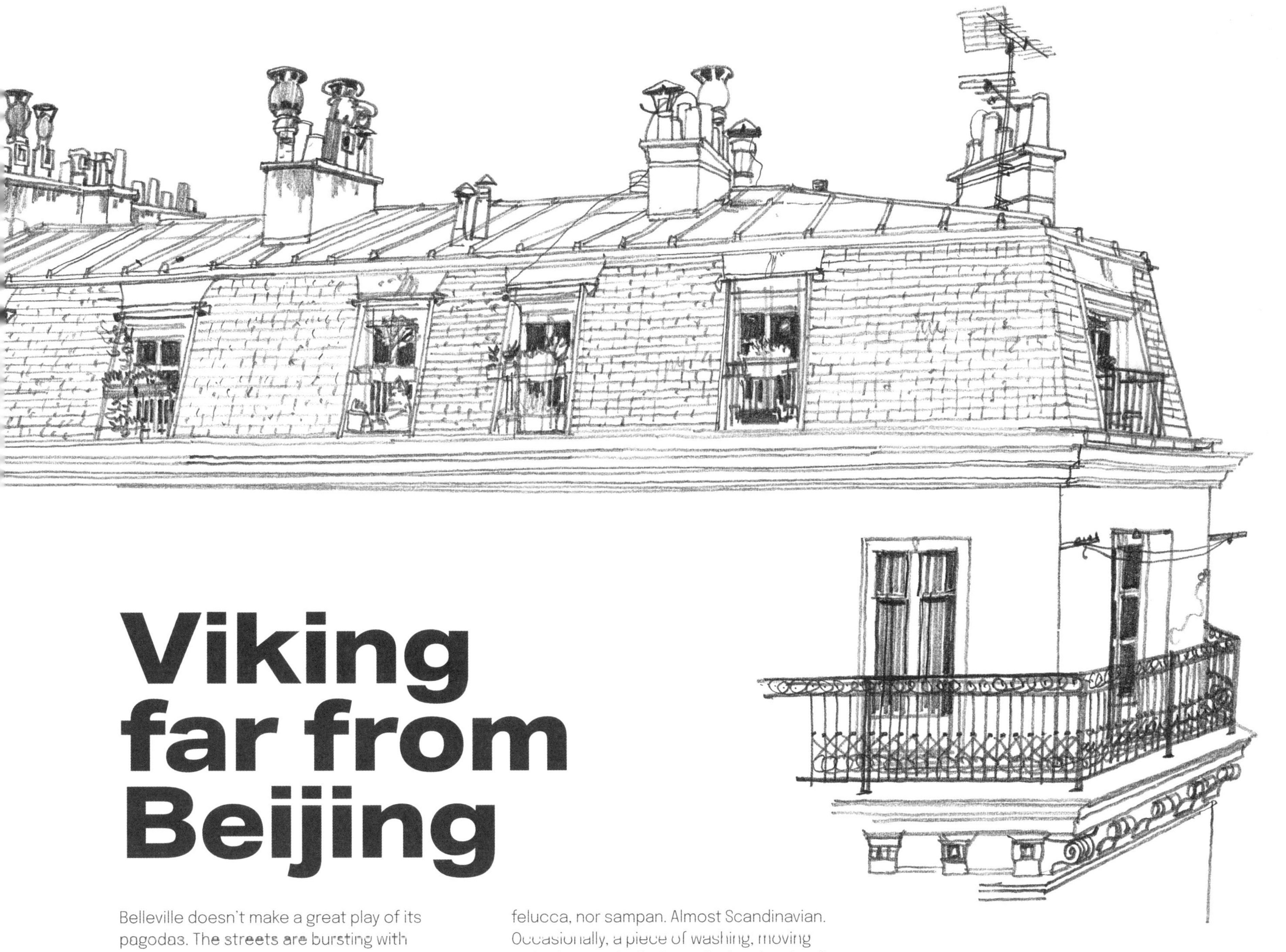

Viking far from Beijing

Belleville doesn't make a great play of its pagodas. The streets are bursting with colour while the roofs temper the lights, the laughter and fleeting songs, with their range of blue-greys, their dulcet litany of faded slate. Rue Civiale is like a perfect upturned ark, with flowering balconies, a ship apparently silent, neither junk, nor felucca, nor sampan. Almost Scandinavian. Occasionally, a piece of washing, moving in the breeze, looks for its haiku. The sky all around waits for a kite that never comes. We dream of watching it float away, bright and eye-catching, and wrapping itself around the Eiffel Tower that, at night, seems to turn slowly into a giant neon tube.

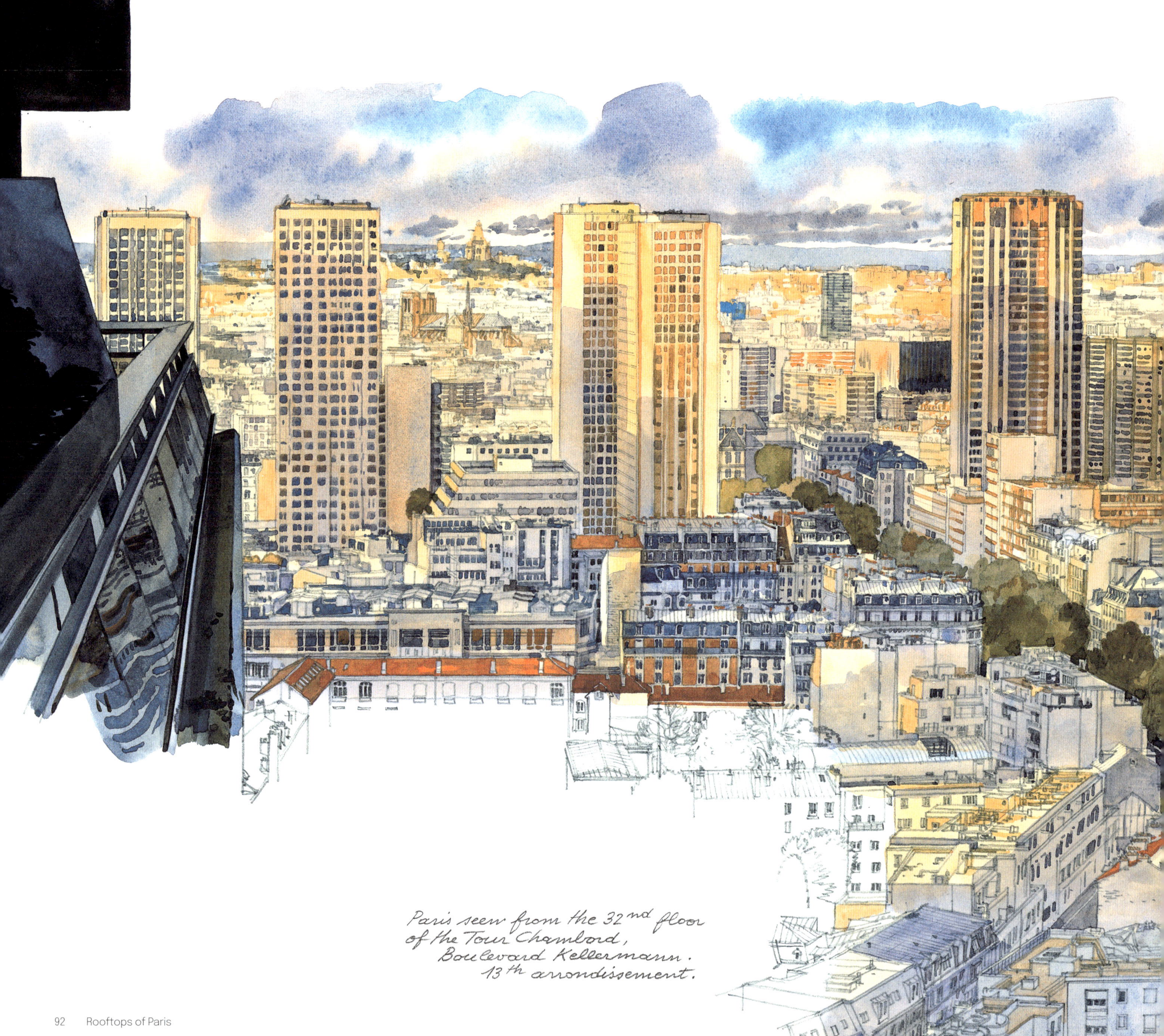

Paris seen from the 32nd floor
of the Tour Chambord,
Boulevard Kellermann.
13th arrondissement.

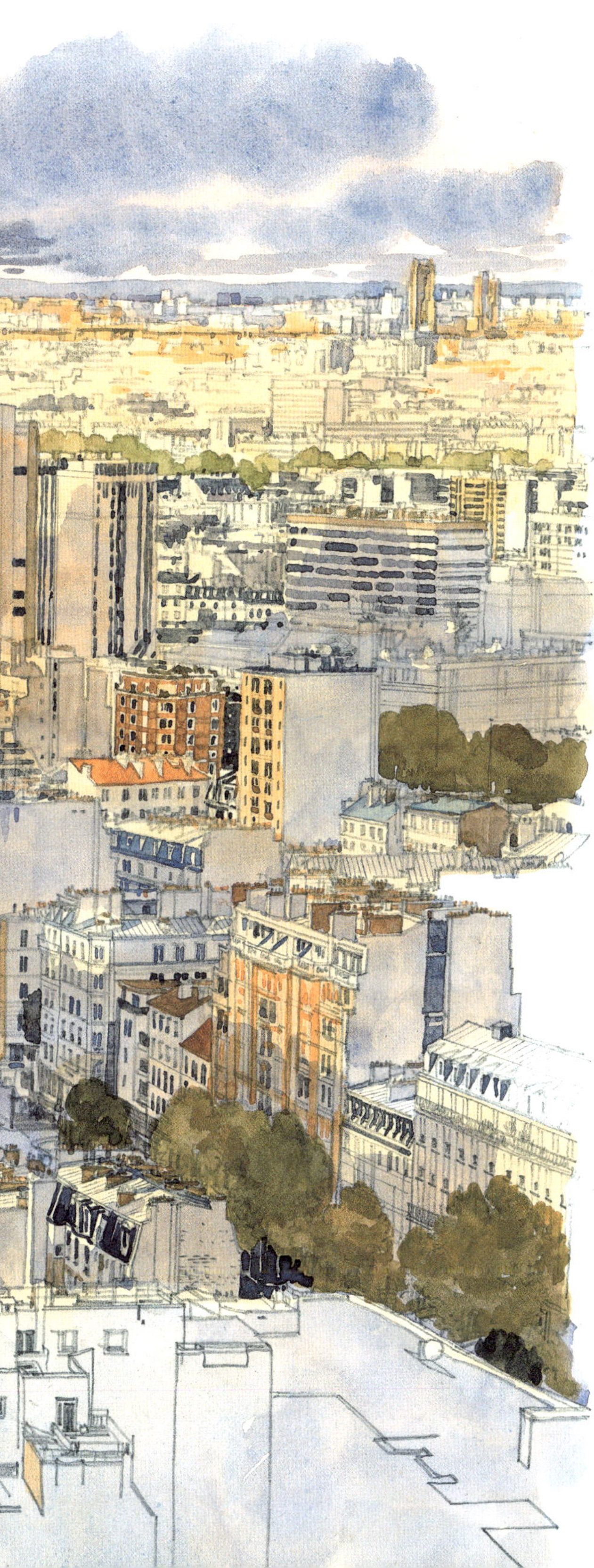

Tower blocks and detours

There are some roofs that fill us with dreams. There are others that have let themselves go. You can fall a long way from not very high. You can also aspire to a bit of sky at your window, to enjoy the sun, to stretch out carelessly, even at the risk of falling, just for the pleasure of being by yourself for a moment. As we come upon the tower blocks of the 13th arrondissement, we can see the great wide world beyond, and this book draws to a close.

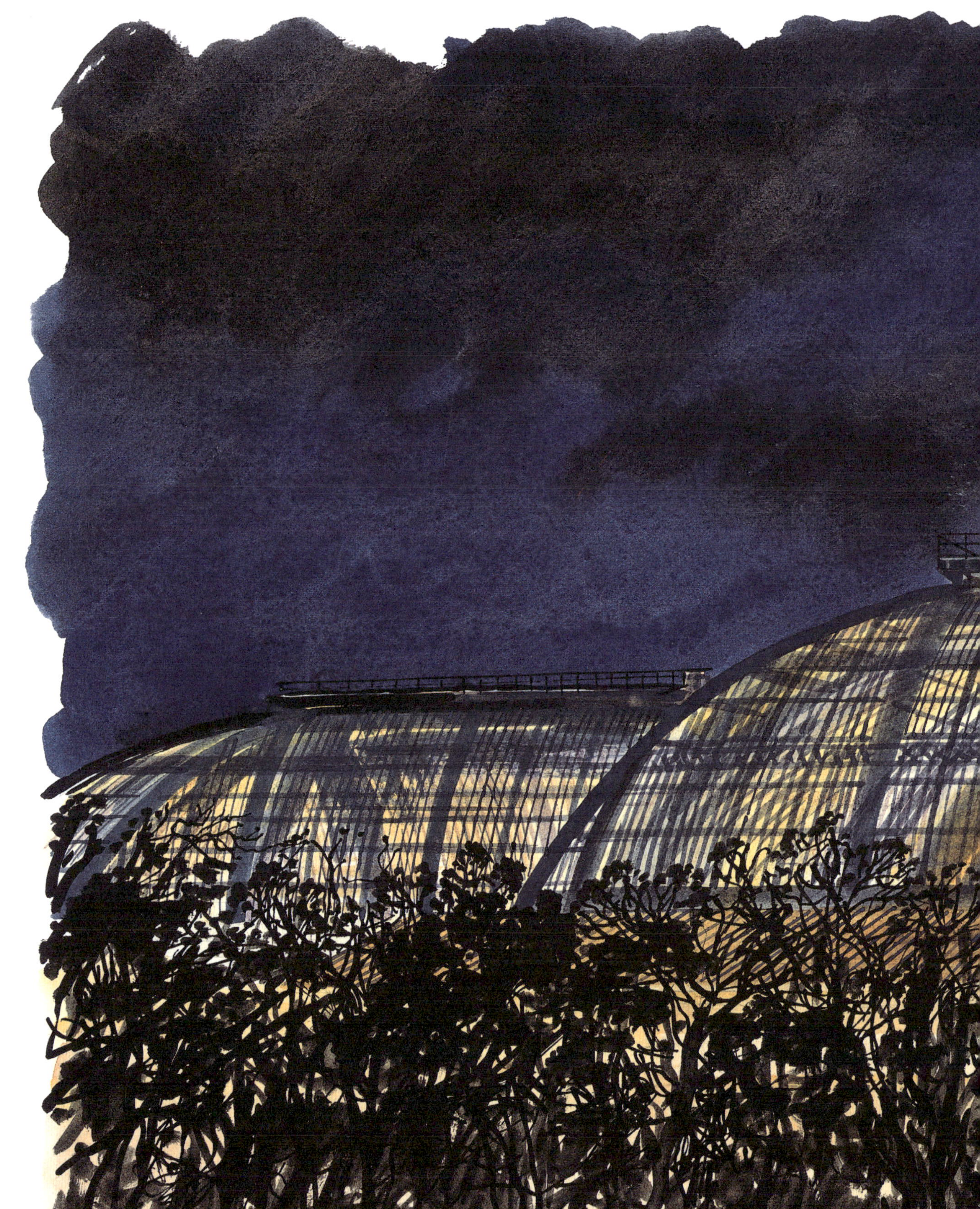

The glass roof of
the Grand Palais.
8th arrondissement.

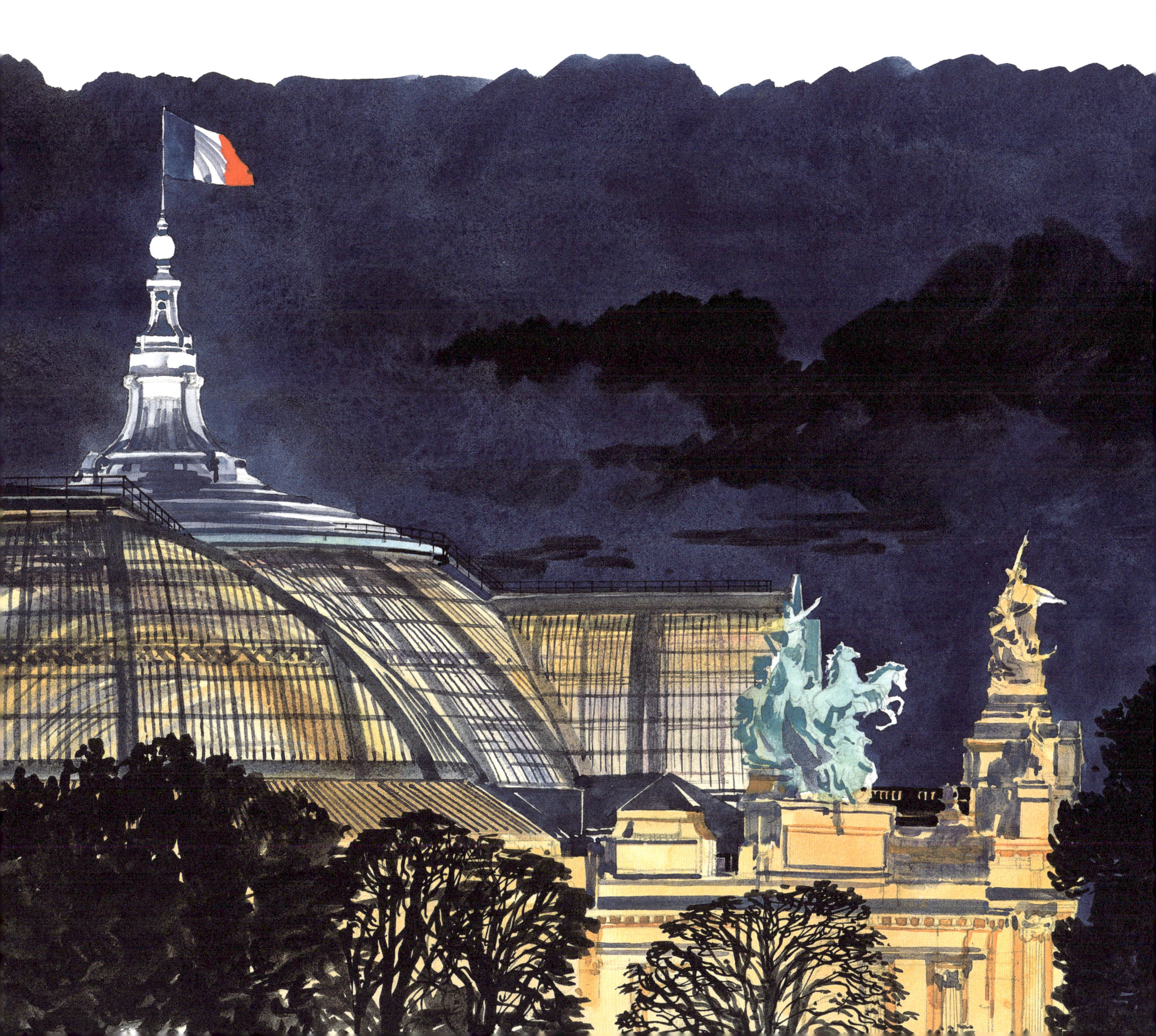

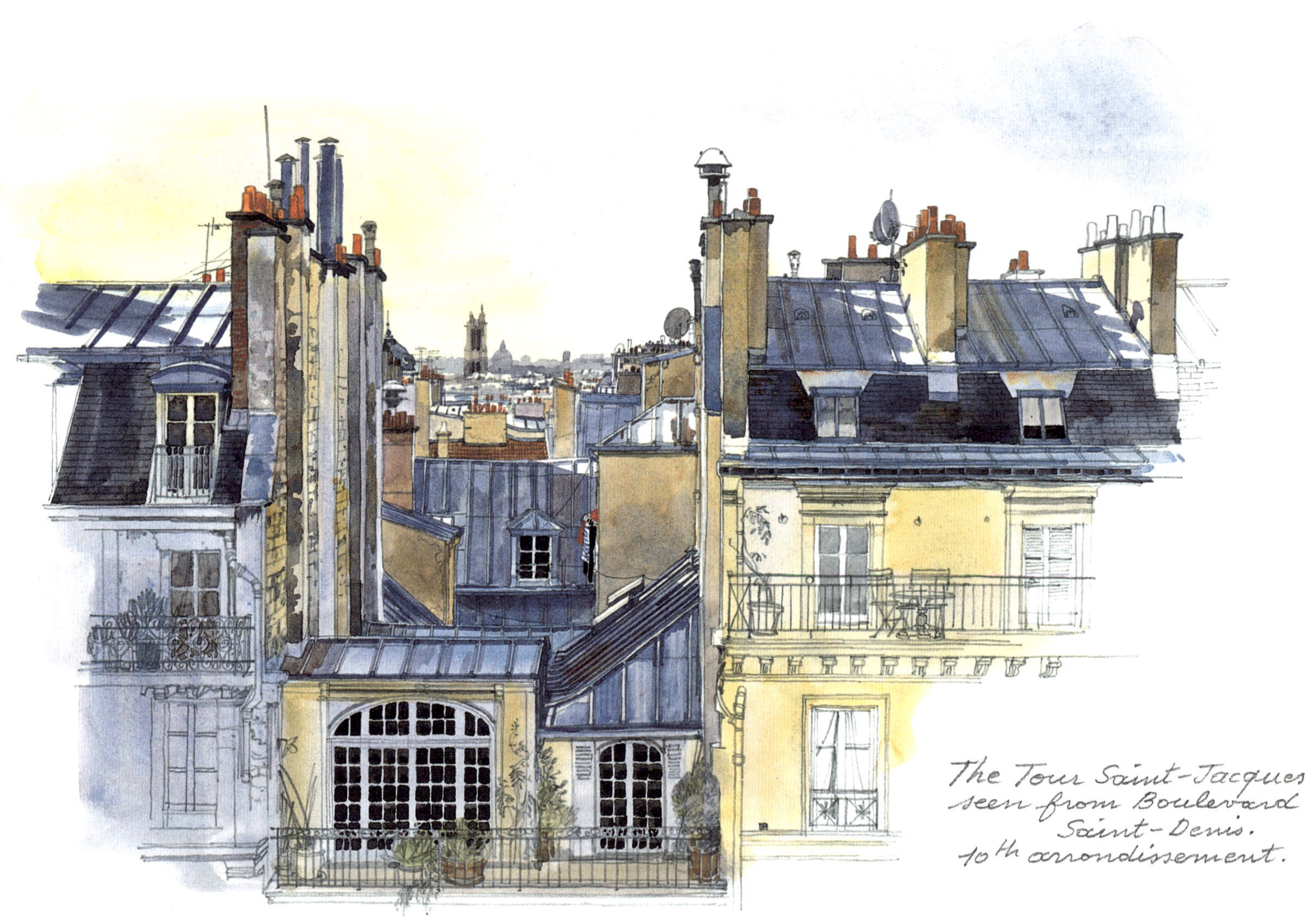

The Tour Saint-Jacques
seen from Boulevard
Saint-Denis.
10th arrondissement.

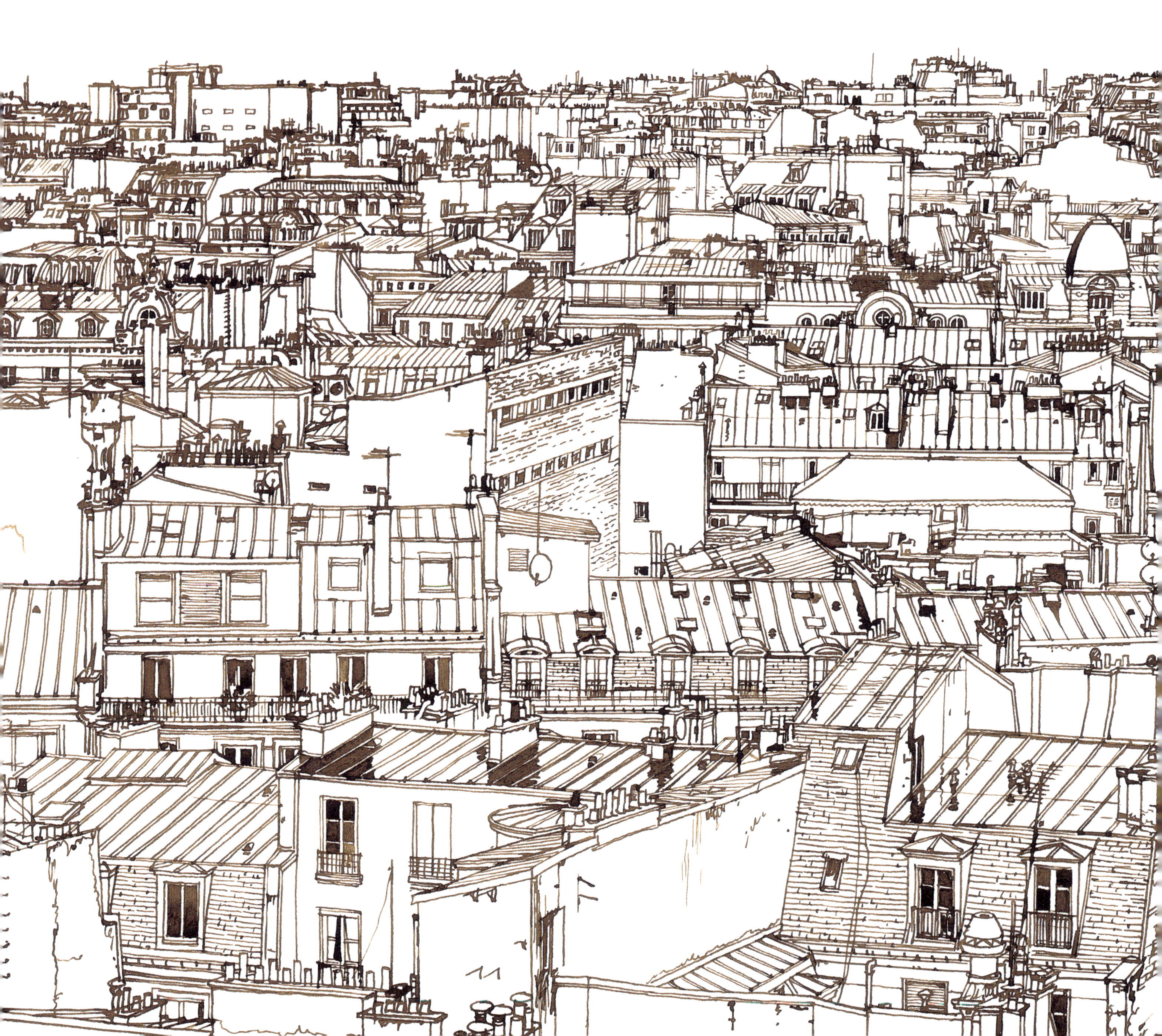